Nonfiction—Grade 4
Table of Contents

Nonfiction
Grade 4

Introduction

Instilling in reluctant readers the desire to read can be one of the most difficult tasks for an educator. Success—having your once reluctant reader *ask* for books—can be one of the most rewarding experiences a teacher can have.

The stories in this book have been written with one purpose. They are all written to capture and hold the interest of all readers—whether they think they like to read or not. These stories are also nonfiction. Good readers who may not normally choose nonfiction to read will find these stories irresistible. They will learn that nonfiction stories can be as exciting, mysterious, thrilling, and moving as any piece of fiction. These stories tell of courage, hard work, strength, commitment, faith, hope, luck, sorrow, happiness, and mystery. They begin with a hook that draws the reader in. Then they tell their story quickly so the reader does not lose interest. Before they know it, students have read *with interest* and *learned* from nonfiction!

Organization

The stories in this book fall into eight categories: Challenges, Rescues, Firsts, Adventures, Mysteries, Escapes, Disasters, and Heroes. Each category has between two and six stories.

Each story is followed by four short activities to test students' comprehension. The activities are titled *Do You Remember?*, *Exploring Words*, *Critical Thinking*, and *Express Yourself*. *Do You Remember?* asks literal questions and requires the student to distinguish between true and false statements. Students will also find multiple choice questions in this section. *Exploring Words* helps students with vocabulary through cloze, completing sentences, finding like meanings, and crossword puzzles. The *Critical Thinking* exercises include cause and effect, fact and opinion, main ideas, sequence, and drawing conclusions. *Express Yourself* includes letter writing, writing news articles, journal entries, and creative writing. Students will draw conclusions and use their abilities for extending and evaluating meaning as they write.

There is a Progress Chart on Page 6. If this is distributed to the students, they can keep track of how they are doing on the exercises. You will note that for the *Express Yourself* exercises, it is suggested that the teacher give a score of 1 to 5, 5 being the best score for the writing.

Use

Nonfiction is designed for independent use by students. Copies of the stories and activities can be given to individuals, pairs of students, or small groups for completion. They can also be used as a center activity.

To begin, determine the implementation that fits your students' needs and your classroom structure. The following plan suggests a format for this implementation.

1. **Explain** the purpose of the activities to your class.

2. **Review** the mechanics of how you want students to work with the stories and exercises. Do you want to introduce the subject of each article? Do you want to tap into the students' prior knowledge of the subject and create a word web?

3. **Do** a practice activity together. Review with students how to use context to figure out the meaning of a word. Remind them to use a dictionary when the context is not enough to figure out the meaning.

4. **Determine** how you will monitor the Assessments. Each assessment can be given individually, or all four pages can be given as a pre-test and a post-test. If given individually, you may give one page before the students begin to work with the book, one or two at the halfway point, and one or two after completion of the book. Tests can be administered individually, to a group that has successfully completed the activities, or to the whole class. The tests are not meant to determine students' knowledge of the content of all the stories, but to determine students' abilities to draw information from nonfiction writing.

5. **Assure** students that this work is for practice purposes. Through this work they will become better readers in all subjects. Go over the Letter to Students with them and answer any questions that arise.

Additional Notes

1. **Parent Communication** Use the Letter to Parents, and encourage students to share the Letter to Students with their parents. Decide if you want to keep the activity pages and Assessments in portfolios for conferencing, or if you want students to take them home as they are completed.

2. **Bulletin Boards** Display selected research projects and writing assignments in your classroom.

3. **Have Fun** Encourage students to discuss the stories and their reactions to them. Encourage any constructive debate or discussions of personal experiences that may arise from the reading.

Dear Parents:

Our class will be working with a book of nonfiction reading. The book has 28 stories of real-life challenges, rescues, firsts, adventures, mysteries, escapes, disasters, and heroes. They were written to interest every reader. Even students who do not read often will enjoy these exciting stories. If students are interested, they will get more out of their reading. It also helps students to talk about their reading. Ask your child about what he or she is reading and share your own knowledge about the events.

Each story is followed by exercises to test students' understanding of their reading. These exercises and the reading may be done in class or at home. If your child brings work home, please consider the following suggestions:

- **Provide a quiet place to work.**
- **If your child is reading, help your child find the meanings of difficult words through the context of the story. Discuss the story.**
- **Go over the directions for the exercises together.**
- **Check the lesson when it is complete. Note areas of improvement as well as concern.**

Thank you for being involved in your child's learning. Your efforts will encourage your child and promote a lifelong love of learning.

Cordially,

Dear Student:

Our class is going to be working with a book of exciting real-life stories. These stories are all real, and they are all amazing. There are mysteries, heroes, challenges, and rescues. There are adventures, escapes, disasters, and firsts.

Find out what happened when two men went to the deepest part of the ocean for the first time. Read about miners buried in a mine, and a little boy who saved his mother by not giving up. Learn about the first men to reach the North Pole, and a mysterious monster in a Scottish lake. Learn about survival on a raft in the middle of the ocean and a fire that could not be put out.

After each story, there are some short exercises. These will tell you how well you read. Chances are you will remember these interesting stories. Read carefully, and you will do well. You may take them home as homework. Remember to work in a quiet place. Work away from the television and radio. You will be able to concentrate on your work.

Happy Reading!

Cordially,

Name_____   Date_____

Nonfiction Grade 4
Progress Chart

Story Titles	Do You Remember?	Exploring Words	Critical Thinking	Express Yourself	Your Score
Saving the Children			X		__/18
Exploring Challenger Deep			X		__/20
Dogsleds to the Rescue				X	__/17
Trouble on the Mississippi			X		__/19
Miracle at Springhill				X	__/18
Survival in the Yukon			X		__/15
Pulled from the Potomac			X		__/20
The Little Boy Who Could			X		__/15
Circling the World				X	__/14
Man's First Flight				X	__/14
Reaching the North Pole			X		__/19
The Swim of a Lifetime				X	__/15
Amazing Voyage			X		__/16
Around the World				X	__/18
Joy Adamson				X	__/15
Tracking Bigfoot			X		__/20
A Monster in the Lake				X	__/13
House of Terror				X	__/13
No Lock Could Hold Him			X		__/15
Alone on a Raft				X	__/15
Crash Landing!			X		__/15
Fire! Fire! Fire!				X	__/14
A City Under Snow			X		__/18
A Mountain Erupts			X		__/20
A Park in Flames				X	__/14
A Pirate's Last Stand				X	__/15
Voice for the Children				X	__/12
Teacher with a Dream				X	__/14

To Find Your Score:

1. Count the number of correct answers you have for each activity.

2. Write these numbers in the boxes in the chart.

3. Ask your teacher to give you a score (maximum of 5) for **Express Yourself.**

4. Add up the numbers to get a final score.

Assessment 1
Nonfiction Grade 4

Directions: Read the selection. Then complete the exercise below.

Ralph Flores was flying his plane from Fairbanks, Alaska, to Seattle, Washington. His only passenger was Helen Klaben. A snowstorm made it impossible for Ralph to see where he was going. The plane crashed into some trees in the forests of the Yukon. This is an uninhabited area of Northern Canada.

Both Ralph and Helen were badly injured. They had very little food. The nearest road was 60 miles away and the temperature was -48°. Both Helen and Ralph had lost their boots in the crash. They had no sleeping bags or blankets. But Ralph and Helen did not give up.

Weeks and weeks went by. Helen and Ralph ran out of food. They were in pain from their injuries and they were frostbitten. But they helped each other. They never gave up trying to make contact with passing airplanes. Finally, when Ralph stamped out the letters SOS in the snow, they were spotted. Rescue workers could not believe that they had lasted 49 days in the freezing wilderness.

Directions: Choose the best ending for each sentence. Write the letter in the blank.

_____ **1.** Helen and Ralph's plane crashed in a
   a. lake.   b. large meadow.   c. forest.

_____ **2.** Both Helen and Ralph were
   a. pilots.   b. angry.   c. injured.

_____ **3.** The temperature was
   a. -48°.   b. 40°.   c. 0°.

_____ **4.** Helen and Ralph ran out of
   a. firewood.   b. food.   c. money.

_____ **5.** They were rescued when Ralph
   a. walked to a road. b. made smoke signals.   c. stamped out SOS.

Assessment 2
Nonfiction Grade 4

Directions: Read the selection. Then complete the exercise below.

It was April 1909. Robert Peary and Matthew Henson were making their eighth attempt to reach the North Pole. They wanted to be the first men to reach it. This would be their last chance to try. Peary's body was wearing out from the cold and the Arctic sun. Henson was an African American. In 1909, people would not support an African-American explorer. When Peary quit, Henson would have to quit, too.

They took 4 men and 133 dogs. They had to hurry. If the weather got warmer, the ice might melt. They were hundreds of miles out on the frozen Arctic Ocean. If the ice weakened, they would all drown. Mile after mile, they trudged north. On April 4, they ran into trouble. There was a break in the ice. A thin layer of new ice had formed, but it was not as strong. Peary crossed first, and then Henson. Then the dogs crossed. But as the next man tried to cross the ice, it cracked. He sank to his knees and crawled across. There was one more man. He crawled across, too. Finally, they were all safe. They moved on, exhausted.

Two days later, they were only 35 miles from the pole. Matthew Henson went ahead to make a trail. When Peary caught up with Henson, he smiled. "I think I'm the first man to sit on top of the world," Henson said. Peary took out an American flag. "I have been waiting for years to do this," he said, and stuck the flag in the snow.

Directions: Pretend that you are Robert Peary or Matthew Henson. You have just reached the North Pole. Write a letter to a friend telling him or her how you feel. Use the back of this paper or another sheet if you need more room.

Dear _____,

_____

_____

_____

_____

_____

Assessment 3
Nonfiction Grade 4

Directions: Read the selection. Then complete the exercises below.

Poon Lim was on board a British ship during World War II. A German submarine shot a torpedo at the ship. Twenty-five-year-old Poon Lim found himself in the ocean. The ship was sinking. He swam toward a raft from the ship. He looked around. He was the only survivor.

There was a little food and water on the raft. There were also some flares. Poon Lim knew the food would not last long. He used his fishing skills to get more food. He hung up the fish he caught to dry so they would last. He found a way to collect fresh water. He sang songs to cheer himself. One day he saw a ship and fired his flares, but the ship did not see his signals. Then the fish stopped biting. Poon Lim ran out of food.

One day Poon Lim noticed the water turning brown. He was near land! Soon afterward, a fishing boat picked him up. Poon Lim had drifted halfway across the Atlantic. He had survived 133 days at sea!

A. Directions: Number the sentences to show the order in which things happened in the story.

_____ Poon Lim ran out of food.

_____ Poon Lim noticed that the water was turning brown.

_____ Poon Lim's ship was hit by a torpedo.

_____ Poon Lim tried to get the attention of a passing ship.

_____ Poon Lim caught fish to eat.

_____ Poon Lim was rescued by a fishing boat.

B. Directions: Write *fact* or *opinion* next to each sentence.

_____ **1.** Poon Lim should not have been on the ship that was sunk.

_____ **2.** Poon Lim was an experienced fisherman.

_____ **3.** Poon Lim survived many days on the ocean.

_____ **4.** Poon Lim was very brave.

Assessment 4
Nonfiction Grade 4

Directions: Read the selection. Then complete the exercises below.

Every year Sam Strong held a meeting. The people at the meeting all shared something in common. They all survived the Blizzard of '88.

Sam Strong was 10 years old when the blizzard hit. The people of New York did not realize how serious the storm was. They thought it would end soon. Sam's aunt bundled him up and sent him to school. Icy snow drove into his face and down his neck. He could hardly see. Minutes later, Sam was lifted from the sidewalk by the wind and thrown into a deep snowdrift. He struggled to get out, but he could not move. He began to panic. He thought he would die in the snow. Finally, a policeman passing by heard Sam's cries. He dug into the snow and found Sam. He sent Sam home.

It took Sam hours to get back home. But he was lucky. Nearly 300 people died in that storm. In the freezing snow and wind, sparrows fell dead in the streets, frozen. Horses died, too. Snowdrifts were 20 feet and higher. It was a storm Sam Strong and many others would never forget.

A. Directions: Write the best ending for each sentence.

1. Sam's aunt sent him to school in the storm because _____.

2. Sam could not see because _____.

3. Sam was in the snowdrift because_____.

4. Sparrows and horses lay dead in the streets because _____.

B. Directions: Write *true* or *false* in front of each sentence.

_____ **1.** Sam was thrown into a snowbank by the wind.

_____ **2.** Sam could have gotten out of the snow by himself.

_____ **3.** The storm was just a small one.

_____ **4.** Nearly 300 people were killed in the blizzard.

_____ **5.** Snowdrifts were 30 feet high.

Saving the Children

Doctor Sara Josephine Baker walked through a poor neighborhood in New York City. As she turned the corner, she saw a long line of people coming toward her. Most were crying. A few carried flowers. At the head of the line, four men held a small white coffin. "Another life has ended," she thought sadly. "Another baby has died."

Dr. Baker knew that dozens of babies died in New York City every day. They were born to women in the poorest neighborhoods. When the summer heat hit, the milk in their bottles spoiled. Bugs crawled on their skin. The babies weren't strong enough to fight disease. In the summer of 1907, 1,500 babies died in New York City each week.

"Once the babies get sick, it's too late," Dr. Baker thought. "I must find a way to keep them from getting sick in the first place." Dr. Baker believed that most diseases could be prevented. She said, "Babies need clean clothes, fresh air, good milk. If they have those things, then most healthy babies will stay healthy."

Dr. Baker worked for the city's health department. The department had little extra money to prevent disease. Besides, preventing disease was a strange new idea. In 1908, doctors just took care of people who were already sick. Dr. Baker remembered that 30 nurses worked for the city schools. They were free in the summer. Why not use them to teach young mothers about health? Dr. Baker got the city to agree to the idea. In June 1908, she explained her plan to the nurses.

"We're going to the Lower East Side," she said. "We will visit every family with a new baby. These families have no way to keep milk from getting sour." Dr. Baker reminded the nurses, "So tell them they don't have to buy milk. Have them try breastfeeding instead. Tell them to give their babies more baths. Their buildings are very hot, with almost no fresh air. Tell mothers to take their babies for walks every day."

The families tried Dr. Baker's ideas. They were amazed. Their babies were not dying. They were not even sick! Dr. Baker's plan was working. By the end of the summer, she had saved the lives of 1,200 babies. That August, Dr. Baker was asked to be the head of a new government office. It was the first government office ever to deal with child health.

Saving the Children (p. 2)

In 1911, she took another step. Dr. Baker opened 15 milk stations. These stations sold good fresh milk at very low prices. In 1911 alone, the milk stations saved the lives of 1,000 babies.

In 1911, Sara Josephine Baker turned her attention to foundlings. These babies' parents had died or left them. In 1911, one out of every two foundlings died.

"What is wrong?" Dr. Baker asked herself. "These babies live in hospitals. They are kept clean and warm. They are fed good food. Why are so many of them dying?"

Dr. Baker saw that only one thing was missing from their lives: love. She said, "These babies need to be held and cuddled and loved." At that time, most experts believed that children should not be given much love. They thought it would spoil children. But Dr. Baker believed she spoke the truth. In 1912, Dr. Baker set up a foster parent program for foundlings. The babies were taken out of the hospital. They were put in homes with loving mothers. By January of 1913, Dr. Baker announced that this program was a success.

In just five years, Dr. Baker had made a big difference in New York City. For the next 30 years, Dr. Baker kept working to keep children healthy. When she died in 1945, she had saved the lives of thousands and thousands of babies.

Do You Remember?

Read each sentence below. Write _T_ if the sentence is true. Write _F_ if the sentence is false.

_____ **1.** Dr. Baker worked in Chicago, Illinois.

_____ **2.** In 1908, doctors just took care of people who were already sick.

_____ **3.** Dr. Baker believed babies didn't need fresh air.

_____ **4.** The milk stations saved the lives of many babies.

_____ **5.** Dr. Baker believed that too much love would spoil a baby.

12

Saving the Children (p. 3)

Express Yourself

Pretend that you are the mother or father of a baby. You live in the Lower East Side of New York in 1911. Dr. Baker's ideas have saved your baby's life. On a separate piece of paper, write a letter to Dr. Baker telling how you feel about her.

Exploring Words

| foster | disease | prevented | mothering |
| foundlings | coffins | cuddled | department |

Use the words in the box to complete the paragraphs. Reread the paragraphs to be sure they make sense.

Dr. Sara Josephine Baker often saw small white **(1)** _____ being carried through the streets of New York City. This made her very sad. Dr. Baker began sending nurses to visit poor families. She **(2)** _____ the deaths of many babies. She taught mothers how to keep healthy babies from getting a **(3)** _____ which could kill them. Many mothers listened to her. Their babies stayed well.

In 1908, Dr. Baker left her job at the city health **(4)** _____. She became head of a new government office. Here Dr. Baker worked to help **(5)** _____. She took them out of hospitals and put them in **(6)** _____ homes. She believed that love was an important part of **(7)** _____. Experts did not agree. But Dr. Baker proved that babies needed to be **(8)** _____.

Exploring Challenger Deep

"Do you think we should go ahead with the dive?" Don Walsh asked. Jacques Piccard thought for a moment. The sea was becoming rough. High waves washed across the deck of the *Trieste*. In addition, some minor instruments were broken. But if they stopped now, they would have to put off the dive for months. Jacques Piccard made his choice.

"I'm going to check things out," he said. "If the main equipment is in order, we shall dive immediately."

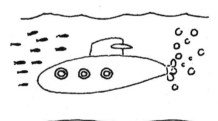

It was dawn on January 23, 1960. Piccard and Walsh were aboard the bathyscaph *Trieste*. A bathyscaph is a special boat that can dive deep under water. The *Trieste* had taken some deep dives before. But this time Piccard planned to take it to the deepest known place in the world. The spot is called Challenger Deep. It is seven miles straight down in the Pacific Ocean. That makes it one mile deeper than the world's highest mountain is high. As Piccard and Walsh got ready, the high waves continued. The two men bounced around inside the bathyscaph.

There wasn't much room. Their cabin measured just three feet across and six feet high. "Can we really make it?" Piccard wondered. "We have to be right on target. If we are not, we'll crash into underwater cliffs before we reach the bottom."

At 8:23 A.M. Piccard gave the signal. The dive began. The *Trieste* sank slowly at first. Then it picked up speed. For a while Piccard could see some light coming through the windows. Then there was darkness. Piccard and Walsh saw tiny plants and animals glowing in the dark. These things gave off their own light, like fireflies in the night.

Piccard and Walsh were all alone. An underwater telephone was their only tie to the main ship. "9:20, depth 2,400 feet," reported Piccard. "We have entered a world of eternal darkness."

As expected, the temperature inside the *Trieste* dropped. Piccard and Walsh put on warm clothing. At 4,200 feet they spotted a leak. Drops of water ran down the wall. Luckily, it soon stopped.

The *Trieste* kept dropping. It passed the 18,000-foot mark, then the 24,000-foot mark. Walsh glanced at Piccard. "We are at a depth where no one has yet been," he said. Piccard just nodded.

Piccard turned on the searchlight. There was no sign of life anywhere.

© Steck-Vaughn Company

Stories of Challenge
Nonfiction 4, SV 6179-6

Exploring Challenger Deep (p. 2)

As the *Trieste* approached Challenger Deep, Piccard slowed it down. Then, suddenly, Piccard and Walsh heard a dull cracking sound. The cabin began to tremble. The two men looked at each other in fear. Had they hit the bottom too fast and too soon? "Have we touched bottom?" asked Walsh nervously.

"I don't think so. The depth finder hasn't shown anything," answered Piccard.

They waited and listened. They heard nothing else. Then Walsh discovered that a window had cracked.

"In my opinion," said Piccard, "it isn't anything serious. Let's go on and we'll see later."

At 12:56 P.M. Piccard said, "Don, look. Here is the bottom."

"Finally," whispered Walsh.

At 1:06 P.M. the *Trieste* made a perfect landing on the bottom of the ocean. There Piccard and Walsh took some measurements. From a window, they watched a fish swim by. "There is life this far down," thought Piccard in amazement. After 20 minutes, the *Trieste* began its slow climb back to the surface of the ocean. When they arrived, Piccard and Walsh were tired, but happy. They had done what no one else had done. They had viewed the deepest part of the ocean with their own eyes.

Do You Remember?

Read each sentence below. Write *T* if the sentence is true. Write *F* if the sentence is false.

_____ **1.** There was an underwater telephone on the *Trieste*.

_____ **2.** A window in the *Trieste* cracked during the dive.

_____ **3.** Walsh and Piccard found life at the bottom of the ocean.

_____ **4.** The *Trieste's* searchlight broke at the bottom of the ocean.

_____ **5.** Walsh and Piccard were the first people ever to reach the bottom of Challenger Deep.

Name_____   Date_____

Exploring Challenger Deep (p. 3)

Express Yourself

Pretend you are Jacques Piccard. You are about to make the dive to the bottom of the ocean. On a separate piece of paper, write a letter to a friend explaining why you are willing to risk your life to reach Challenger Deep.

Exploring Words

Choose the correct word from the box to complete each sentence.

in addition	eternal	immediately	searchlight	minor
bathyscaph	opinion	amazement	equipment	depth

1. *Also* means the same thing as _____.

2. Things that have a special use are called _____.

3. If you do something right away, you do it _____.

4. Something that is less important is _____.

5. If something goes on forever, it is _____.

6. We call a measure of how deep something is _____.

7. The feeling of being amazed is _____.

8. A belief is an _____.

9. A special boat that can dive deep under water is a _____.

10. A very bright light is a _____.

Stories of Challenge
Nonfiction 4, SV 6179-6

Dogsleds to the Rescue

Dr. Curtis Welch stared at the sick young boy. He had a fever, and his throat was swollen. Every few minutes he broke into a deep cough. Dr. Welch shook his head and muttered, "Diphtheria. He and many others will die if we don't get medicine soon. Diphtheria spreads very quickly."

Dr. Welch was worried. Most people who came down with diphtheria died. There was a cure—a medicine called antitoxin. But Welch didn't have any. There wasn't any for miles around. He feared the disease would kill everyone in the frozen town of Nome, Alaska.

The next day, January 27, 1925, Dr. Welch sent a message to other Alaskan cities. He needed antitoxin fast.

The nearest antitoxin was in Anchorage, about 900 miles away. All the roads were closed for the winter. Planes couldn't fly because of the winds and cold. The railroad tracks only came as far as Nenana, which was over 650 miles from Nome.

The governor of Alaska decided the antitoxin should be sent by railroad from Anchorage to Nenana. From there, it would be carried by relay teams of dogsleds. A musher and his dogs would take the antitoxin from Nenana to the next town. The next musher would then take the antitoxin. It would change hands about 20 times before it reached Nome. The plan had to be carried out quickly, or it would be too late.

The trip would be difficult. The mushers and their dogs would face -50°F temperatures, howling winds, and blinding snow. Some of the dogs might not make it. Some of the mushers might not either. Many mushers quickly stepped forward to do the job. They knew it was dangerous. But they knew how to handle their dogs. They knew the way. The mushers were willing to risk their lives to help the people of Nome.

One by one, the mushers carried the antitoxin west toward Nome. All of Alaska watched and waited during this race against time and the weather.

On February 1, the antitoxin reached a small village. It was still over 150 miles from Nome. Here musher Leonard Seppala made a bold decision.

"I'm not going to follow the trail up around Norton Bay," he said. "I'm going to take the shortcut straight across the frozen water."

"In this storm?" one of the townspeople asked. "Those 80-mile-per-hour winds will break up the ice. You and your dogs will fall in and be swallowed up by the water."

But Seppala knew that if he made

Dogsleds to the Rescue (p. 2)

it, he would save precious hours. All around him the snow blew in angry clouds. His dogs slipped on the ice. They groaned. They whimpered. Still he drove them on. At last he reached the other side of the bay.

Gunnar Kasson was the last musher. He had to travel 60 miles to reach Nome. It was 8:00 P.M., and the sky was black. He couldn't wait for morning. He knew that five people had already died. At least 30 more people had caught the disease.

Kasson called to Balto, his lead dog. Balto guided the sled to the snowy trail. Soon the wind grew worse. The freezing air cut through Kasson's heavy winter clothes. It froze his right cheek. His hands ached. The dogs too were in pain. Pieces of ice stuck in their feet. Their paws began to bleed.

And then Kasson lost the trail. The swirling snow had swept away his sense of direction. He prayed that Balto could pick up the scent of the trail again. If not, all was lost. Balto sniffed around in the snow. He turned one way, then another. Soon, Balto picked up speed. He had found the trail!

At 5:36 the next morning, Kasson and his dogs limped into Nome. Kasson collapsed in the snow next to his half-frozen dogs.

"Fine dog," he mumbled again and again. "Balto, you brought us through. You brought us through."

People cheered all the dogs who had made the trip. Kasson and Seppala and the other mushers were heroes. These brave people and their animals had saved the lives of many Alaskans.

Do You Remember?

Read each sentence below. Write *T* if the sentence is true. Write *F* if the sentence is false.

_____ **1.** Dr. Welch was worried.

_____ **2.** The nearest antitoxin was in Montana.

_____ **3.** One man would carry the antitoxin the whole way.

_____ **4.** The journey was dangerous.

_____ **5.** Seppala took a shortcut to save time.

Name _____ Date _____

Dogsleds to the Rescue (p. 3)

Critical Thinking — Cause and Effect ⚡

Complete the following sentences.

1. When Dr. Welch saw that the child had diphtheria, he was very worried because _____.

2. The antitoxin was sent to Nome from Anchorage because _____.

3. Planes couldn't fly because _____.

4. The dogs' paws began to bleed because _____.

Exploring Words 🔍

Read each sentence. Fill in the circle next to the best meaning for the word in dark print. If you need help, use a dictionary.

1. The word **fever** means
ⓐ high body temperature.　ⓑ pain.　ⓒ not as many.

2. The word **swollen** means
ⓐ a river.　ⓑ larger than normal size.　ⓒ sore.

3. The word **diphtheria** means
ⓐ a sickness.　ⓑ a game.　ⓒ a religion.

4. The word **relay** means
ⓐ a kind of race.　ⓑ a smile.　ⓒ slippery.

5. The word **musher** means
ⓐ a meal.　ⓑ a police officer.　ⓒ a dogsled driver.

6. The word **disease** means
ⓐ gasoline.　ⓑ a small animal.　ⓒ an illness.

7. The word **risk** means
ⓐ tear apart.　ⓑ take a chance.　ⓒ remove.

8. The word **collapsed** means
ⓐ fell down.　ⓑ waited.　ⓒ relaxed.

© Steck-Vaughn Company

Stories of Rescue
Nonfiction 4, SV 6179-6

Trouble on the Mississippi

"Tom, bring the _Zev_ up the river from Helena. Don't pile it up on a sandbar. And keep an eye on floating logs," Mr. Hunter ordered.

Tom Lee nodded his head at his boss. He would take the motorboat, _Zev_, up the Mississippi River. He would take it from Helena, Arkansas, to Memphis, Tennessee.

But this would not be an ordinary trip. By the end of the day, Tom Lee would become a hero. He would save 32 people from death.

On May 8, 1925, the river looked peaceful. Lee knew it could be tricky. The spring flood currents were dangerous. But he wasn't worried. He knew how to handle the boat. And he could deal with the currents.

As the _Zev_ moved along, it passed a large steamboat. The steamboat was called the _M.E. Norman_. Lee saw that it was out for a cruise. The men and women on board seemed to be having a good time. Several people waved to Lee. He waved back.

Lee passed the _Norman_. Then he glanced back. "That boat is riding funny," he said to himself. "She's rolling too much to one side to suit me. I'll keep an eye on her."

Lee had pulled about a half-mile ahead of the steamboat. Then it happened. The _Norman_ started to roll crazily. The sun had just gone down. A mist had settled over the river. Lee couldn't see the _Norman_ very well. But he knew it was in trouble. Quickly, he turned the _Zev_ around and raced back down the river.

The steamboat was already on its side and sinking by the time he reached it. Lee could see heads bobbing in the water. He pushed the _Zev's_ motor to full power.

It was getting darker by the minute. And the _Norman_ was far from shore. Lee had no time to waste. As he got closer to the steamboat, it sank out of sight. Lee could see people splashing in the water. He heard cries for help. The swift current was carrying people down the river. Luckily, the _Zev_ had a powerful motor. Lee was able to act in a hurry.

First, he had to get downriver from the struggling swimmers. If he didn't, they would float out of reach. Lee steered the _Zev_ past them. Then he turned around and came back up the river.

Trouble on the Mississippi (p. 2)

Tom Lee moved the *Zev* slowly through the dark water. Again and again he stopped and pulled people into his boat. Soon the *Zev* was full. Lee brought the frightened people to the shore 300 feet away.

Then Lee went back to find others. Luckily, some of the passengers were strong swimmers. Seventeen of them managed to swim to the shore safely. Others held on to life preservers or pieces of wood. All were drifting down the river.

Lee got as many as he could. He made five trips between the shore and the river. He saved 32 people. Lee helped them make a fire on shore. Then he spent the rest of the night searching the river. He was trying to find more people. In all, 23 drowned.

James Wood was one of the 32 passengers saved by Tom Lee. "If it had not been for Tom Lee, I would not be here today. I owe my life and my wife's life to him."

When asked about the rescue, Lee said he just happened to pass the sinking boat. He said he did what anyone else would have done in his place. But to the people on the *Norman*, Tom Lee was not just an ordinary person. He was a brave and skillful man who had meant the difference between life and death.

Do You Remember?

Read each sentence below. Write *T* if the sentence is true. Write *F* if the sentence is false.

_____ **1.** Lee's boss told him to take the *Zev* up the river.

_____ **2.** Lee had never been out on the Mississippi before.

_____ **3.** Some people on the *Norman* were strong swimmers.

_____ **4.** Lee quit looking for people when it got dark.

_____ **5.** Thirty-two people were saved by Lee.

Trouble on the Mississippi (p. 3)

Express Yourself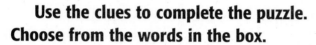

Imagine that you are a reporter writing about the boat accident and Tom Lee. Use a separate piece of paper. Tell who, what, where, when, and why in your newspaper article.

Exploring Words

Use the clues to complete the puzzle.
Choose from the words in the box.

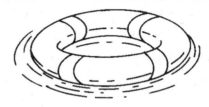

bobbing
cruise
currents
death
life preservers
mist
powerful
sandbar
struggling

Across

4. very strong
7. moving bodies of water
8. a light rain
9. moving up and down

Down

1. things used to keep people from drowning
2. a boat ride taken for fun
3. trying hard
5. the end of life
6. ridge of sand on the bottom of a river

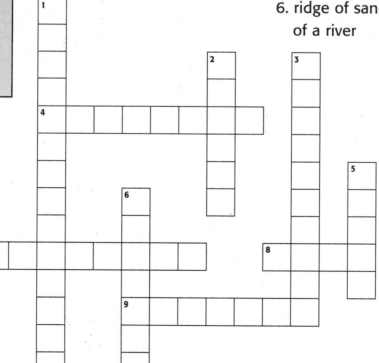

Miracle at Springhill

The miners of Springhill knew the risks. Mining was tough, dangerous work. Over the years, hundreds of men had died in the mines. Others became sick from breathing coal dust. But the small Canadian town of Springhill was a mining town. If a young man wanted a job, he worked in the mines as his father and grandfather had.

On October 23, 1958, the earth shook violently. This sudden movement of the earth was called a "bump."

This bump trapped 174 men in the mines. Eighty-one were quickly rescued. Twenty-four others were known dead. That meant the remaining 69 men were still trapped 4,000 feet straight down.

For the next six days, rescue workers tried to dig down to the trapped miners. But it was a very deep mine. The digging went slowly.

Family and friends waited day after day. They stood around the entrance to the mine. They prayed for good news. Slowly, they began to lose hope. By the morning of October 29, most people had stopped coming to the mine. Families started planning church services for their lost men.

Rescue workers kept digging. But by the sixth day, they had no real hope of finding anyone alive.

On the afternoon of October 29, a rescue worker uncovered the top of a 60-foot pipe. He heard a voice. It was coming from the far end of the pipe! "There are 12 of us in here. Come and get us."

The 12 men were stuck in a space only four feet high. They had not eaten food or breathed fresh air for days. Yet somehow, they were still alive.

Three of the miners had lived through a bump two years before. These men knew what to do. They helped the others stay calm.

The 12 men searched for food. They found a few lunch boxes that contained water and sandwiches. They tried hard to keep their spirits up. They told jokes, sang songs, and prayed aloud.

After three days, the food was gone. So was most of the water. The air grew stale. Every few hours the miners thought they heard rescue workers. They yelled for help. But they never got an answer. They found an air pipe and took turns tapping out SOS on it. But they feared the pipe was broken and their efforts useless.

Miracle at Springhill (p. 2)

After six days, the miners were weak. They were terribly hungry and thirsty. But they kept tapping on the pipe. Suddenly, they heard a sound from the other end of the air pipe. Tears formed in the miners' eyes. They were going to be saved!

Up above, the good news flashed through the town. Doctors and more diggers rushed to the mine. Families and friends also came running.

The rescue workers dug quickly. They got within 20 feet of the miners. But they found they could go no farther.

"We have to go back out and start again," one of the diggers shouted down the pipe.

But it was only a short delay. The digging went on. At last, after 13 hours, rescue workers reached the survivors. In a short time, all 12 men were safely out of the mine.

Two days later the rescue workers found seven more miners alive. All the buried miners had been given up for dead. But 19 of them had survived. To the people of Springhill, this rescue really was a miracle.

Do You Remember?

In the blank, write the letter of the best ending for each sentence.

_____ **1.** For the first few days, families of the trapped men waited
    ⓐ near the mine.   ⓑ at church.   ⓒ in a hotel.

_____ **2.** The miners tapped out SOS on
    ⓐ a rock.   ⓑ an air pipe.   ⓒ a lunch box.

_____ **3.** Three of the trapped miners had lived through an earlier
    ⓐ bump.   ⓑ hurricane.   ⓒ flood.

_____ **4.** While trapped in the mine, the miners told
    ⓐ ghost stories.   ⓑ jokes.   ⓒ tall tales.

_____ **5.** After six days, the miners were
    ⓐ wet.   ⓑ dead.   ⓒ rescued.

© Steck-Vaughn Company

Stories of Rescue

Nonfiction 4, SV 6179-6

Miracle at Springhill (p. 3)

Critical Thinking — Fact or Opinion?

A *fact* can be proven. An *opinion* is a belief. Opinions cannot be proven. Write *F* before each statement that is a fact. Write *0* before each statement that is an opinion.

_____ **1.** Being a miner is no fun.

_____ **2.** Some miners were killed in the bump on October 23, 1958.

_____ **3.** Friends of the trapped miners gave up hope too soon.

_____ **4.** The 12 miners should have tapped on the pipe more often.

_____ **5.** The 12 men all made it out of the mine alive.

Exploring Words

Choose the correct word from the box to complete each sentence.

violently	stale	spirits	calm
survivors	miracle	miners	delay

1. When something is no longer fresh, it is _____.

2. People who work in mines are called _____.

3. When people are sad, their _____ are low.

4. People who live through some kind of test or trial are called _____.

5. When something happens with great force, it happens _____.

6. Something that is quiet and peaceful is _____.

7. A wonderful event that can't be explained is called a _____.

8. To put an event off to a later time is to _____ it.

Survival in the Yukon

Helen Klaben stared out the window of the small plane on February 4, 1963. The snowstorm was getting worse. It was hard to see where they were going. They were flying from Fairbanks, Alaska, to Seattle, Washington. But pilot Ralph Flores wasn't sure where they were anymore. He dropped to a lower altitude, hoping to get a clue from the ground.

But this part of Northern Canada, called the Yukon, had no towns. It had only huge, deep forests. Ralph put down his hand to change gas tanks. When he looked up, the plane was headed right for the trees.

The plane crashed through the trees and landed in the snow. Ralph lay slumped against the instruments. Helen, the only passenger in the plane, lay in her seat without moving.

Some time later, they woke up. Blood poured from Ralph's mouth. His jaw was broken. His ribs were smashed. His hands and feet suffered from frostbite. Helen suffered from frostbite, too. Her chin was cut open. And her left arm was badly broken.

It seemed certain they would die. There was no one to help them. The nearest road was 60 miles away. The wind howled, and the snow drifted down through the trees. The temperature was -48°F.

Helen and Ralph had lost their boots in the crash. They had no sleeping bags, blankets, or waterproof clothing. They had very little food. But Ralph and Helen did not give up. They didn't want to die.

They made a small fire next to the plane. They found extra clothes in Helen's suitcase. They tied sweaters around their feet.

Slowly, they cleared out the back of the broken plane. They made a shelter from the cold and wind. That night, they curled up next to each other and tried to sleep.

By the tenth day, Helen and Ralph ran out of food. Now all they had to eat was melted snow and two tubes of toothpaste.

Many times they heard planes flying overhead. A few times they even saw planes. They built fires and flashed mirrors. They tried to make radio contact. But none of the planes noticed them.

By the 32nd day, they gave up hope that anyone would find them in the forest. They had to get to a clearing where they could signal passing planes. Ralph set out to scout the area. He told Helen he would be back in three days.

Survival in the Yukon (p. 2)

About a mile away, he found a clearing. So he built a shelter and waited. He waited for eight long days, but no planes came.

Helen was so happy to see Ralph when he returned to the plane that tears ran down her cheeks. They had now been in this frozen forest for 40 days.

They knew they had to try again to get help. This time Helen would also go. Her feet were still in bad shape from frostbite. So Ralph spent a few days making a sled for her to ride on. Then he began dragging it down a hill. The sled kept tipping over, so finally Helen got out and walked. The snow came up to her waist. She lost the sweaters that had been wrapped around her feet. She was sick to her stomach. Ralph's whole body ached. He had stomach cramps. But somehow they kept moving.

At last they came to a large clearing. Ralph made a fire and boiled snow to make water for them to drink. He built a new shelter out of tree branches. Then he and Helen lay down to sleep. They were exhausted.

Several days later, Ralph decided that the clearing was not big enough. He wanted to find a larger field. Slowly, he traveled alone four miles to a huge meadow.

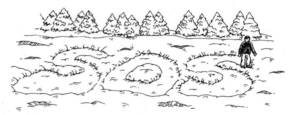

There he stamped out the letters SOS in the snow. Then he made an arrow that pointed toward Helen's shelter. A bush pilot named Chuck Hamilton saw the letters. He called the police. And so, 49 days after the crash, rescuers found Ralph and Helen.

Some rescue workers were shocked that Helen and Ralph were still alive. They didn't think that anyone could last more than two weeks in such hostile conditions. But both Helen and Ralph had the will to live. They helped each other, and they never gave up.

Express Yourself ✎

Pretend that you are Helen Klaben. Your plane has crashed in the Yukon. It has been 40 days, and still you have not been rescued. On a separate piece of paper, write an entry in your journal describing your thoughts, hopes, and fears.

Survival in the Yukon (p. 3)

Do You Remember?

In the blank, write the letter of the best ending for each sentence.

_____ **1.** Helen and Ralph's plane crashed in a
        a. lake.   b. large meadow.   c. forest.

_____ **2.** In the crash, Helen hurt her
        a. back.   b. left arm.   c. right eye.

_____ **3.** After ten days, Helen and Ralph ran out of
        a. firewood.   b. food.   c. money.

_____ **4.** A pilot finally spotted Ralph's
        a. SOS.   b. smoke signals.   c. jacket.

Exploring Words

Use the words in the box to complete the paragraphs. Reread the paragraphs to be sure they make sense.

smashed	slumped	throbbed	frostbite	cramps	contact

The small plane flew blindly through the clouds. Then the plane

(1) _____ into some trees. When the plane stopped moving, Ralph and

Helen were **(2)** _____ in their seats. They were stuck in a cold,

hostile wilderness.

As the days passed, they grew weaker. They

were cold and wet. Helen's toes turned black with

(3) _____. Ralph's jaw **(4)** _____

with pain. They both had stomach **(5)** _____ from hunger. Finally,

Ralph made **(6)** _____ with a bush pilot by stamping SOS in the

snow. After seven long weeks, they were finally rescued.

Pulled From the Potomac

On January 13, 1982, a huge snowstorm hit Washington, D.C. The airport shut down. Planes waited while snowplows cleared the runways. Two hours later the airport reopened.

Shortly after that, Air Florida's Flight 90 roared down the runway on its way to Tampa. Joseph Stiley was on that plane. He was a pilot himself, and he sensed trouble. The plane didn't climb into the sky the way it should have. Stiley turned to the woman sitting next to him. He said, "We're not going to make it. We're going in."

Many workers had been released early that afternoon because of the snowstorm. At 4:00 P.M., the streets were jammed with people going home. Traffic was at a standstill on the 14th Street Bridge.

Suddenly, a blue and green plane dropped out of the sky. Lloyd Creger was one of the people on the bridge. He watched in horror as the plane dropped. "It was falling from the sky, coming right at me," said Creger. "It hit the bridge and just kept on going like a rock into the water."

Leonard Skutnik was a 28-year-old office clerk. He was in one of the cars on the bridge. Skutnik and many other people got out of their cars and rushed to the scene.

The plane's tail had ripped the tops off several cars. Four people sitting in cars had been killed. The plane itself had plunged into the icy Potomac River.

Skutnik was stunned. He and the others watched in silence as the plane disappeared. Only the tail stayed above the water. Of the 79 people aboard, only six could be seen. These six held on to the tail with all their strength. They had to be rescued fast. Some of them were badly injured. No one could stay in the freezing water long without dying.

A rescue helicopter arrived and went to work. It lowered a ring to the water. One person grabbed it and was dragged to the shore. Then a second person was pulled to safety.

Next it was Priscilla Tirado's turn. She was weak and half-frozen. She could hardly reach for the ring. A man in the water next to her helped her. It was Stiley, the off-duty pilot. He was one of the six who had survived the crash. He was in trouble, too. Both his legs were broken. Still, he managed to help Tirado catch the ring.

Tirado tried to hold on as the helicopter dragged her out of the water. But she was too weak. The ring slipped from her hands. She fell back into the icy river.

Back on shore, Leonard Skutnik and the others stood watching. They saw Tirado fall into the water. Skutnik stripped off his shoes and jacket. He plunged into the river. He swam out 25 feet to Tirado. She was so weak and cold she couldn't struggle anymore. Skutnik grabbed her and swam back to shore. When he got close to the bank, a firefighter swam out to help him. Together they carried Tirado to safety.

Skutnik became a hero overnight.

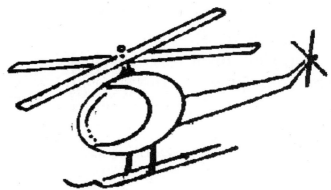

His rescue was shown again and again on the news.

But Skutnik didn't see himself as a hero. He said, "Nobody else was doing anything. I just did it."

In the end, five of the six people in the water were saved. Joseph Stiley survived. So did one flight attendant. And because of Leonard Skutnik's brave act, so did Priscilla Tirado.

Do You Remember?

In the blank, write the letter of the best ending for each sentence.

_____ **1.** Air Florida Flight 90 crashed in
   a. the summer.   b. Alaska.   c. the winter.

_____ **2.** The plane fell into
   a. a park.   b. a river.   c. an office building.

_____ **3.** When the crash occurred, Leonard Skutnik was in
   a. the plane.   b. a boat.   c. his car.

_____ **4.** Priscilla Tirado had trouble hanging onto
   a. her hat.   b. the ring.   c. a police officer.

_____ **5.** A ring was lowered into the water by a
   a. firefighter.   b. helicopter.   c. doctor.

© Steck-Vaughn Company

Stories of Rescue

Nonfiction 4, SV 6179-6

Pulled From the Potomac (p. 3)

Express Yourself

Pretend that you are Joseph Stiley. On a separate piece of paper, write an article for a magazine. Describe your experiences on January 13.

Exploring Words

Use the words in the box to complete the paragraphs. Reread the paragraphs to be sure they make sense.

runway	plunged	jammed	horror	off-duty
sensed	injured	released	clerk	stunned

Air Florida Flight 90 roared down the **(1)** _____. A few moments after takeoff, it crashed. It hit a bridge **(2)** _____ with cars and then **(3)** _____ into the Potomac River. People who saw the plane go down were **(4)**_____. They watched in **(5)** _____ as the plane sank.

Only six people lived through the crash. One of the six was Joseph Stiley, an **(6)** _____ pilot. Stiley was badly **(7)** _____. Still, he helped Priscilla Tirado grab a rescue line. But she was too weak to hold the line. She **(8)** _____ it and dropped back into the water. Back on shore, an office **(9)** _____ named Leonard Skutnik **(10)**_____ that she was in trouble. Skutnik jumped into the water and rescued her.

The Little Boy Who Could

Kelley Lyons lay trapped inside the wrecked pickup truck. Pain shot through her arms. The sharp edge of the door cut into her head.

Under Kelley lay her five-year-old son, Rocky. He had been asleep when the accident took place.

"Look, Mama," he said. "The car's upside-down, and the wheels are pointing toward the sky."

Kelley tried to look, but her face was covered with blood. Panic rose inside her. She thought she was blind.

It was early Halloween morning, 1987. Kelley Lyons was not a reckless driver. She knew that this back road in western Alabama could be dangerous. She always took extra care going around the turns. But this night she didn't see the giant pothole in the road.

At 12:40 A.M., Kelley's truck hit the pothole. A tire stuck in the hole. That caused the truck to flip over. It bounced off the road and down a 20-foot slope. Kelley threw herself on top of Rocky to protect him. When the truck stopped rolling, it was upside-down. Kelley and Rocky were trapped inside.

As Kelley lay there, she thought about her husband, Marty. He was in New York now, getting ready for a big football game. He wasn't home to notice that she and Rocky hadn't arrived.

Suddenly, Kelley smelled gasoline. She feared the truck would burst into flames. "You've got to get out of here," she told Rocky.

Rocky crawled out the truck window. Then he came back and reached for Kelley.

He tried to pull her out. But it was no use. Rocky weighed only 55 pounds. He stood four feet two inches tall. Rocky decided to try something else. He got behind Kelley. He pushed until he got her out of the truck.

Kelley was relieved to be out of the truck. But she was still at the bottom of the ravine. She knew she was badly hurt. She had to get help.

Rocky offered to climb up the bank and stop a car. But Kelley said no. She was afraid he might be hit.

"Come on, Mom. I can help you get up the hill. I can push."

Slowly, they began crawling up the steep hill. Rocky got behind Kelley and pushed.

Inch by inch they moved up the steep ravine. By the time they got halfway up the hill, Kelley was ready to quit. She was in terrible pain.

© Steck-Vaughn Company

Stories of Rescue

Nonfiction 4, SV 6179-6

The Little Boy Who Could (p. 2)

"I can't go any further," she whispered. In the darkness, Rocky hugged his mother. He remembered a children's story Kelley often read to him. It was *The Little Engine That Could*. In the story, a little train tries to climb a huge mountain. The train keeps saying, "I think I can, I think I can."

"Mommy, you've got to remember the train. You know, 'I think I can, I think I can.'"

Kelley thought about what Rocky was saying. He was right. She couldn't give up now. Slowly, she began struggling up the hill again.

At last Rocky and Kelley reached the top of the ravine.

In a few minutes, a truck passed them and then turned around and came back. The woman drove them to the nearest hospital.

There Kelley discovered that she was not blind. But her face was badly cut. The bones in both shoulders were shattered. Doctors bandaged her arms. They performed an eight-hour operation to repair her face. It took over 200 stitches.

The hospital called Kelley's husband, Marty Lyons. He flew home immediately. Both Kelley and Marty are very proud of their son. Kelley is sure that she would have bled to death if Rocky had not been there to help her. His courage helped save her life.

Express Yourself ✐

Pretend you are Rocky Lyons. On a separate piece of paper, tell a friend about the accident. How did you feel? What did you do?

The Little Boy Who Could (p. 3)

Do You Remember?

In the blank, write the letter of the best ending for each sentence.

_____ **1.** The accident occurred in
     a. New York.   b. Alabama.   c. Hawaii.

_____ **2.** Kelley was afraid the truck was going to
     a. burst into flames.   b. sink.   c. get wet.

_____ **3.** Rocky remembered a story about a little
     a. circus elephant.   b. mouse.   c. train.

_____ **4.** Kelley feared the accident had damaged her
     a. eyes.   b. truck.   c. suitcase.

Exploring Words

Read each sentence. Fill in the circle next to the best meaning for the word in dark print. If you need help, use a dictionary.

1. Kelley was **relieved** to be out of the truck.
   ⓐ sad and depressed   ⓑ happy   ⓒ worried

2. The truck rolled down into a **ravine**.
   ⓐ street   ⓑ open meadow   ⓒ ditch

3. Rocky showed **courage** in helping his mother.
   ⓐ silly thoughts   ⓑ good manners   ⓒ bravery

4. The accident **shattered** several of Kelley's bones.
   ⓐ colored   ⓑ broke   ⓒ froze

5. Kelley's face **bled** from the many cuts.
   ⓐ blushed   ⓑ lost blood   ⓒ broke

6. Kelly was not a **reckless** driver.
   ⓐ perfect   ⓑ damaged   ⓒ careless

Circling the World

Ferdinand Magellan held his breath. He couldn't wait to hear what King Charles V of Spain would say to him.

"I have read your request," the king said. "But I am not sure I understand. Do you want to sail to the Spice Islands?"

"Yes, Your Majesty," said Magellan. "If you let me use your ships, I will find a faster and easier way to reach the Spice Islands. I will bring the spices back to Spain."

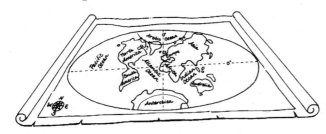

The king nodded. "I see. But the Spice Islands lie to the east. Why do you plan to sail west?"

"The earth is round," said Magellan. "If I sail west, sooner or later I will end up in the east."

The King asked many questions. No one had ever sailed around the world. In March 1518, King Charles decided to help Magellan. "I will give you five ships," he said. "But you must find your own crew."

Magellan needed 250 men. Some of his crew were brave and trusted sailors. But Magellan also signed up criminals. They went just to get out of jail.

Magellan set sail in September of 1519. It took his ships two months to cross the Atlantic Ocean. They ran into many storms. At last they reached South America. There they turned south and followed the coast. They were searching for a water passage.

Soon Magellan's men became tired and unhappy. Winter was coming. The men wanted to go home. Magellan would not turn around. "I will die before I will turn back," he said. "We will anchor for the winter. In the spring, we will continue our journey." Some men planned to take over. Magellan put an end to that trouble. But he knew it could happen again.

For five months Magellan waited for spring. One of his ships was destroyed in a storm. At last he set off again. On October 21, 1520, Magellan saw a wide opening along the coast. He turned his ships into it. It would later be named the Strait of Magellan.

For the next 38 days, Magellan's ships made their way through a tangle of rocks. At times the passage was very narrow. It twisted one way, then another. The men were afraid. On the supply ship the men gave up. Without telling Magellan, they turned around and sailed home. With them went most of the food.

On November 28, Magellan finally

© Steck-Vaughn Company

Stories of Firsts

Nonfiction 4, SV 6179-6

Circling the World (p. 2)

saw open water up ahead. He wept with joy as his ships sailed out into a beautiful blue sea. This ocean seemed so gentle. The men named it the "Pacific." This means the peaceful sea.

Magellan thought the Pacific was about 600 miles wide. He thought he would reach the Spice Islands in a few weeks. In fact, the Pacific Ocean is over 11,000 miles wide. Day after day he stared into the distance, hoping to see land. But he saw only water.

After two months of this, the group was in terrible shape. The ships creaked and groaned with each wave. New leaks appeared every day. The men had no fresh food. Many of them became sick.

At last, the Spice Islands were only a few hundred miles away.

"I've done it!" Magellan thought happily. "I've found a route all the way around the world."

His men wanted to get home. But they became caught in a war. In a battle on April 27, 1521, Magellan was killed.

The men were very sad.

Juan Sebastian del Cano took command. He sailed the three ships on to the Spice Islands. There he decided that  only one ship could go on. On September 8, 1522, this ship finally reached Spain. Del Cano fell to his knees in thanks when he saw land. He had lived through the amazing voyage around the world. He was one of only 18 men who had made it.

Critical Thinking — Main Ideas

Underline the two most important ideas from the story.

1. Magellan tried to reach the Spice Islands by sailing west.

2. Some of Magellan's crew members were criminals.

3. Magellan found a route that led all the way around the world.

4. The men on the supply ship headed back to Spain without telling Magellan.

Circling the World (p. 3)

Do You Remember?

Read each sentence below. Write *T* if the sentence is true. Write *F* if the sentence is false.

_____ **1.** Magellan hoped to reach the Spice Islands by sailing west.

_____ **2.** The men on the supply ship decided to sail back to Spain.

_____ **3.** Magellan knew the true size of the Pacific.

_____ **4.** Only 18 of Magellan's men made it back to Spain.

Exploring Words

Use the clues to complete the puzzle. Choose from the words in the box.

Word Box
anchor
criminals
Majesty
passage
request
rare
spice
vitamin C

Across
2. helps keep bodies healthy
7. a place you can pass through
8. something asked for

Down
1. hard to find
3. people who break the law
4. what a king or queen is called
5. keeps a ship in the same place
6. adds flavor to food

Man's First Flight

"Look at those birds," sighed Orville Wright. "They make it look so easy."

"Yes," agreed his brother, Wilbur. The two brothers stood on the porch of their home in Dayton, Ohio. They were watching a couple of hawks circling in the sky.

"There must be a way for us to fly," said Orville. "If we worked hard enough, I bet we could build a flying machine."

"Well, there's only one way to find out," said Wilbur. "Let's give it a try!"

The Wright brothers were very good with machines. But they didn't know anything about flying. Still, they believed they could build a self-powered airplane.

In 1899, Orville and Wilbur began reading books on the subject. They read everything they could find. Then they began to experiment on their own.

"First we need to build something that will glide in the wind," said Wilbur. "Later we can add an engine to make it self-powered."

For three years the brothers built gliders. These had wingspans of 17 to 22 feet. They also had space for a pilot to ride lying flat on his stomach. The gliders needed wind to get off the ground. So the brothers traveled to the windy beaches of Kitty Hawk, North Carolina. There they ran many tests. Sometimes their gliders stayed in the air for hundreds of feet. Even so, the men knew something wasn't right.

"Our gliders aren't rising the way they should," Wilbur said.

The brothers went home to Ohio and checked their books. Every one of them said glider wings needed deep downward curves. The Wright brothers had built their glider wings according to these directions. Now they began to wonder if the books were wrong.

To find out, the Wrights built their own wind tunnel. It had a fan that blew air through a small tunnel. The Wright brothers used this to test over 100 sets of wings. Each set had a different curve. When they completed their tests, they knew the answer. The books were definitely wrong.

"The next glider we build will have only a slight curve to its wings!" said Orville firmly.

In 1902, the Wrights again traveled to Kitty Hawk. Their new glider, with its gently curving wings, did beautifully. Now there was just one thing left to do — add an engine.

© Steck-Vaughn Company

Stories of Firsts

Nonfiction 4, SV 6179-6

Man's First Flight (p. 2)

By December 1903, the Wright brothers were ready. They had built a huge plane. It had a 180-pound engine and a wingspan of over 40 feet. It also had a tail and a propeller. On December 17, they took it to a hill overlooking Kitty Hawk's beaches. The spot was called Kill Devil Hills.

At 10:30 that morning, they started the plane's engine. Then, at 10:35 A.M. Orville climbed into the plane. Lying on his stomach, he grabbed the controls. Slowly the plane rose into the air. It reached a speed of seven or eight miles per hour. It flew for 12 seconds and covered 120 feet before landing.

"We've done it!" cried Wilbur as he watched his brother make the world's first flight. "We've really done it!"

Indeed they had. The Wright brothers made three more flights that day. The longest, 852 feet, was made by Wilbur. He was in the air almost a full minute. The Wright brothers had found the secret to building a self-powered plane. The principles they discovered are the same ones used in air travel today.

Do You Remember?

In the blank, write the letter of the best ending for each sentence.

_____ **1.** To get off the ground, the Wright brothers' gliders needed
     ⓐ a push.   ⓑ gasoline.   ⓒ wind.

_____ **2.** The Wright brothers built their own
     ⓐ wind tunnel.   ⓑ train.   ⓒ house.

_____ **3.** The principles discovered by the Wright brothers are
     ⓐ no longer used.   ⓑ all wrong.   ⓒ used today.

Man's First Flight (p. 3)

Critical Thinking — Fact or Opinion?

Write *F* before each statement that is a fact. Write *O* before each statement that is an opinion.

_____ **1.** The beaches of Kitty Hawk, North Carolina, were windy.

_____ **2.** The Wright brothers should have been more careful when testing their plane.

_____ **3.** The Wright brothers' first plane could only carry one person.

_____ **4.** The Wright brothers spent too much time trying to fly.

Exploring Words

Use the words in the box to complete the paragraphs. Reread the paragraphs to be sure they make sense.

self-powered	curves	gliders	
propeller	gently	principles	span

Orville and Wilbur Wright believed they could build a **(1)** _____ flying machine. First they read books to learn the **(2)** _____ of flight. Then they built their own **(3)** _____. These had wings with deep **(4)** _____ in them. They didn't fly well. So the Wright brothers changed the design. They found that the gliders flew better if their wings curved **(5)** _____.

In 1903, the Wright brothers went to Kitty Hawk, North Carolina. They wanted to test their newly–built airplane. The airplane had a wing **(6)** _____ of over 40 feet. It also had a **(7)** _____. On December 17, Orville made the world's first self-powered flight in this airplane.

Stories of Firsts

Reaching the North Pole

Robert Peary and Matthew Henson sat in a small igloo. Outside, wind whipped across the frozen land.

Neither one complained. They were used to this frigid weather. In the Arctic, the temperature often got down to -40 or -50 degrees. Besides, Peary and Henson had something else on their minds.

"We are only 133 miles away," Peary said. "If luck is with us, we should be at the Pole in just a few days."

Peary and Henson had spent 18 years exploring the Arctic. They had made seven trips north. Each time they had been disappointed. They wanted to be the first to reach the North Pole. Now, in April of 1909, they were making one last, desperate attempt.

"No matter how it ends, I will never have another chance," Peary thought to himself. He was 52 years old. The Arctic sun had damaged his eyes. Frostbite had destroyed his toes. He would never make another trip north.

This would be Henson's last trip, too. Henson had started out as Peary's servant. Over time, Henson had learned as much about the Arctic as Peary had. But because Henson was an African-American, he couldn't lead an expedition. In 1909, people would not support an African-American explorer. When Peary quit, Henson would have to do the same.

Peary and Henson headed out. Four Eskimo men and 133 dogs went with them. It was a clear day. The temperature stayed around -25 degrees. Peary pushed the men hard. There was no time to lose. If the weather turned warmer, the ice might melt. They were hundreds of miles out on the frozen Arctic Ocean. If the ice weakened, they would all drown.

Hour after hour, mile after mile, the group trudged north. On April 4, they ran into trouble. Warmer weather had caused a 100-yard break in the ice. A thin layer of new ice had formed. But Peary was not at all sure it would hold the weight of his team.

"I'll cross it first," he announced. "If anyone must risk his life now, it should be me."

Slowly Peary stepped out onto the new ice. It creaked and bent underneath him. Gently he worked his way across. At last he made it to thicker ice.

"Send the dogs over," he called. The dogs made it easily. Then it was time for the other men to cross. "I watched them from the other side

Reaching the North Pole (p. 2)

with my heart in my mouth," Peary later wrote.

Henson and two others crossed without trouble. But as the next man started across, there was a loud crack.

"Get down on all fours!" Peary yelled. "That will spread out your weight!"

Carefully the man sank to his knees. He crawled across the ice on his hands and knees. When he arrived safely, the last man crawled across.

That night everyone was exhausted. Peary checked their position. They were only 35 miles from the Pole.

"This is it, my friend," he whispered to Henson. "Tomorrow we should reach the Pole."

Early on the morning of April 6, the group set out. Henson went ahead to make a trail. Finally, he thought he

had gone far enough. When Peary caught up with him, Henson smiled.

"I think I'm the first man to sit on top of the world," he said to Peary.

After such a long, difficult journey, Peary did not know what to say. He made a quick check of their position. Then he reached into his pack and took out a wrinkled American flag. "I have been waiting for years to do this," he said, and stuck the flag in the snow. They had reached the North Pole.

Do You Remember?

Write *T* if the sentence is true. Write *F* if the sentence is false.

_____ **1.** In the Arctic, the temperature often got down to -40 or -50 degrees.

_____ **2.** Henson had not learned nearly as much about the Arctic as Peary had.

_____ **3.** Peary was the first to cross a patch of thin ice.

_____ **4.** Henson was the first to reach the North Pole.

Reaching the North Pole (p. 3)

Express Yourself

Pretend you are Robert Peary or Matthew Henson. You have just reached the North Pole. On a separate piece of paper, write a letter to a friend telling him or her how you feel.

Exploring Words

Use the clues to complete the puzzle. Choose from the words in the box.

igloo
frigid
Arctic
frostbite
expedition
trudged
layer
underneath
exhausted
position

Across

2. a sheet of something
5. very tired
6. walked slowly and heavily
7. what happens when parts of a person's body freeze
8. a house built of ice or snow
9. beneath

Down

1. where something is placed
3. area around the North Pole
4. a group of people who travel for a special reason
7. very cold

The Swim of a Lifetime

Gertrude Ederle had been swimming for almost nine hours. She was more than halfway across the English Channel. If she finished this swim, she would be the first woman ever to swim from France to England.

"It looks good," thought her trainer, Bill Burgess. He was riding in a tugboat next to 18-year-old Trudy, as Gertrude was called. Suddenly he saw a huge wave hit her. She stopped swimming. Her head went under water. "Help her!" Burgess called wildly to one of his men. "She's going to drown!"

Instantly the man swam to Trudy and grabbed her. "I was just stopping to get the salt water out of my mouth," Trudy cried.

But it was too late. To make an official swim across the Channel, a swimmer could not be touched by anyone along the way.

The English Channel is over 20 miles wide. Its salt water is cold and rough. Also, the tides and currents in the Channel are strong. They can sweep even the best swimmer out to sea.

"I'm going to try again," Trudy told her father, Henry "Pop" Ederle.

"Good," Pop said. "When you make it across, I will buy you your own car."

On August 6, 1926, Gertrude Ederle stood again on the French side of the English Channel. She wore a pair of goggles. She was covered with three coats of grease to keep her body from losing heat. At 7:09 that morning, she waded into the water at Cape Griz-Nez.

A little way off shore, a tugboat was waiting for Trudy. In it were Bill Burgess, Pop Ederle, and several friends. They planned to stay with her as she made her swim.

For the first three hours, Trudy faced rough waters. Still, she moved quickly. At noon, Burgess hung a baby bottle over the side of the boat. It contained clear chicken soup. He also dropped her a chicken leg. Trudy ate, then kept swimming.

That afternoon the wind kicked up. The water became rougher. Trudy slowed down a bit. But then she reached the halfway point. She heard

The Swim of a Lifetime (p. 2)

her friends singing "The Star-Spangled Banner." Trudy felt a new rush of energy. She even began to sing along with them.

At 3:50 P.M. she called to Burgess. "How much longer before I reach England?"

"About five hours," he answered.

"Don't forget that car, Trudy!" Pop shouted out.

"I won't!" she called back. "I'll be driving it in just a few days!"

Over the next three hours, the storm grew worse. Rain poured down. The wind howled. The waves became stronger. At 6:05 P.M. Burgess shook his head. "We've got to get her out," he said to Pop. "No one can keep swimming in this weather."

"Come out!" he yelled to Trudy.

"What for?" Trudy called. Her tongue was swollen from the salt water. Her whole body was battered from the rough seas. But her body and her spirit were still strong.

At 7:35 P.M. she finally reached the in-shore tide. The waves were now helping to sweep her toward shore. At 9:30 P.M. she saw lights on the beaches of England. Thousands of people clapped and cheered as Trudy swam toward them. At 9:35 P.M. she reached the shore of Dover, England. She had done it! She had crossed the English Channel. In doing so, Trudy had swum 35 miles. And she had beaten the world's record for the crossing by over two hours.

Critical Thinking — Finding The Sequence

Write *1* before the sentence that tells what happened first in the story. Write *2* before the sentence that tells what happened next, and so on.

_____ Burgess told Trudy to come out of the water.

_____ Trudy reached the shore of Dover, England.

_____ Burgess dropped Trudy a chicken leg.

_____ Trudy heard her friends singing "The Star-Spangled Banner."

_____ Trudy waded into the water at Cape Griz-Nez.

The Swim of a Lifetime (p. 3)

Do You Remember?

In the blank, write the letter of the best ending for each sentence.

_____ **1.** The water in the English Channel is
     ⓐ deep and still.   ⓑ filled with sharks.   ⓒ cold and salty.

_____ **2.** Trudy's father promised that when she made it across, he would
    buy her a
     ⓐ house.   ⓑ horse.   ⓒ car.

_____ **3.** To keep her body from losing heat, Trudy was covered with
     ⓐ grease.   ⓑ wool.   ⓒ lotion.

_____ **4.** During her swim, Trudy ate
     ⓐ a chicken leg.   ⓑ a steak sandwich.   ⓒ nothing.

Exploring Words 🔍

Write the correct word in each sentence.

official	swollen	currents	energy	tides	battered

1. Something that counts for a record is _____.

2. The rise and fall of the oceans are called _____.

3. If something is hit over and over again, it is _____.

4. Areas of water in an ocean that move in a certain direction are _____.

5. Something that is _____ has become larger than usual.

6. To be able to do work is to have _____.

Amazing Voyage

Captain William Bligh lay asleep in his cabin on the _H.M.S. Bounty_. It was just before dawn on April 28, 1789. Suddenly the door swung open. Fletcher Christian stood in the doorway. Christian grabbed the captain and pulled him out of bed.

"I'm taking control of the ship," snarled Christian. "Don't make another sound, or I'll kill you right now."

This was called a mutiny. Death by hanging was the punishment. Christian didn't care. He hated Captain Bligh.

Christian dragged Bligh out of his cabin. Several other men helped him. They forced Bligh into a small, open boat along with 18 of the crew members who refused to join the mutiny. Slowly the _Bounty_ sailed away from the small boat. It seemed certain they would die. They were in the middle of the Pacific Ocean. The nearest friendly island, Timor, was 3,800 miles away. Their boat gave them no shelter. It contained only five days' worth of food and water. Captain Bligh felt fear rising inside him. But his men depended on him.

"I won't let these men down," he thought. "I'll do my best to lead them to safety." He told the men they were going to sail all the way to Timor.

"It's a long trip," he warned. "We'll have to ration the food. Every man will get an ounce of bread and a half cup of water each day." The men all agreed.

For the first four days, the weather was clear. On the fifth day, the weather turned bad. Wind and rain tore at the sail. Waves crashed over the boat and filled it with water. Bligh struggled to keep the boat from tipping over. His men bailed water out of the boat. The storm lasted two days. By then the men were exhausted. The bread was wet and had started to rot.

The men tried to stretch out and sleep. But there was not much room. The next day, a new storm blew in. This one lasted 13 days. It seemed that the rain, wind, and lightning would never end.

Bligh could see that his men were losing hope. Their bones ached and their muscles cramped. Everyone was weak. Some were half dead already.

Bligh still hoped to make it to Timor. But he saw that it might take longer than he had planned. They would run out of food. Bligh cut the men's rations in half. It was the only way to make the food last.

By May 25, all the men were near

Amazing Voyage (p. 2)

death. One more cold, stormy night could finish them off. That night the rain stopped. The wind died down. The next day, the sun broke through the clouds. Bligh felt a small burst of hope. Later that day, the men saw birds flying overhead. Surely this meant that land was nearby. The men became more cheerful. When a bird landed on the boat, they grabbed it with their bare hands. This small amount of meat lifted everyone's spirits. It gave them the strength to stay alive.

On May 28, the men spotted land. Bligh warned them not to get too excited. He knew that Timor was still far away.

"We can stop and look for food," he said. "But we must reach Timor before all our strength is gone."

The men gathered coconuts and clams. But soon an angry tribe drove them back out to sea. Once again, they hit rough waters. At night they shivered with cold. In the daytime, the  sun brought new problems. The men became sick from the heat. Their skin burned and peeled. Many also had awful cramps in their stomachs.

At last, after 41 days, Bligh and his men saw Timor. Tears of joy ran down their faces. They were all half starved. Their clothes were rotten, and their bodies were covered with sores. But thanks to Captain Bligh, they had lived through one of the most amazing voyages ever.

Express Yourself

Pretend that you are one of Bligh's men. On a separate piece of paper, write a letter to a friend back home explaining why you refused to join the mutiny.

Amazing Voyage (p. 3)

Do You Remember? 🤔

Read each sentence below. Write **T** if the sentence is true. Write **F** if the sentence is false.

_____ **1.** Fletcher Christian was captain of the <u>H.M.S. Bounty</u>.

_____ **2.** All of the crew members joined in the mutiny.

_____ **3.** Bligh rationed the food.

_____ **4.** Three of Bligh's men died during a storm.

_____ **5.** Birds were a sign that land was nearby.

Exploring Words 🔍

Read each sentence. Fill in the circle next to the best meaning for the word in dark print. If you need help, use a dictionary.

1. Fletcher Christian led the **mutiny**.
　　ⓐ musicians　　　　ⓑ a dance　　　　ⓒ sailors rising up against the captain

2. Captain Bligh had to **ration** the food.
　　ⓐ cook well　　　　ⓑ give out in equal shares　　　ⓒ throw out

3. The men **struggled** during storms.
　　ⓐ argued　　　　　ⓑ worked very hard　　　ⓒ got lost

4. The men **bailed** water for hours without stopping.
　　ⓐ drank　　　　　ⓑ heated　　　　　ⓒ emptied out

5. When they reached Timor, the men were **exhausted**.
　　ⓐ very tired　　　ⓑ angry　　　　　ⓒ happy

6. As the men sat in the boat, their muscles **cramped**.
　　ⓐ became painfully tight　ⓑ grew　　　　ⓒ stretched

© Steck-Vaughn Company

Stories of Adventure
Nonfiction 4, SV 6179-6

Name _____ Date _____

Around the World

Nellie Bly ran up to her editor's office in New York City. Jules Chambers, editor of the newspaper the _World_, had a new assignment for her.

"How would you like to travel around the world?" he asked.

Nellie smiled. "I'd love to!"

"You'd be in a race," Chambers warned.

"What kind of race?" Nellie asked.

"A race against time."

"Against Phineas Fogg's time?"

"Oh, you couldn't possibly beat that."

"Yes, I could," said Nellie. "Just watch me."

In 1872 Jules Verne wrote a story called _Around the World in 80 Days_. Its hero was Phineas Fogg. Fogg won a bet by circling the world in just 80 days. At the time that seemed impossible. But now, in 1889, Nellie Bly wanted to beat Fogg's imaginary record.

Chambers thought it would make a great story. But he didn't really think Nellie could do it. Travel in those days was difficult. The trains were slow. No one knew when a ship might sail.

But Nellie was willing to do anything to get a story. "I'll make it back to New York in just seventy-five days!" she told Chambers.

On November 14, 1889, Nellie sailed for Great Britain. She had never been to sea before. Nellie got seasick the first day. One man laughed at her. He said, "You'll never make it around the world!"

But Nellie quickly got used to sailing. Some of the others were not so lucky. A huge wave washed two sailors overboard. Many passengers got very ill. Even the man who laughed at Nellie became seasick. Finally, after six stormy days, the ship landed in England.

Back in New York, Chambers kept readers informed about Nellie's adventure. He put a map of her route on the front page of the _World_. Fan mail poured in to the newspaper. People wrote songs about Nellie. They named racehorses after her. The newspaper boasted, "The whole civilized world is watching Nellie Bly."

Nellie had to jump onto a moving train in London. She almost missed others. But her plans depended on getting a ship for Asia.

Around the World (p. 2)

In Italy she got lucky. She caught the *Victoria* just as it was about to sail.

In Singapore she saw a small monkey locked in a cage. Nellie's heart nearly broke at the sight. She decided to buy the animal. From then on, the monkey went wherever she went.

On January 7, 1890, Nellie left Japan on board the *Oceanic*. Three days out the weather turned bad. Strong winds and high waves battered the ship. Some sailors blamed Nellie's monkey.

"Your monkey is bad luck," they said. "Throw it overboard!"

Nellie refused. She prayed the storm would end. Then she could still make it to New York on time.

"I can't go back to New York a failure," she thought. "I would rather die than fail."

At last the weather improved, and the ship made it to San Francisco. Nellie and her monkey quickly hopped onto the first train headed for New York. On January 25, she crossed the finish line.

"She's done it!" officials announced. "She's broken Phineas Fogg's record!" Nellie Bly had circled the world in 72 days, six hours, ten minutes and eleven seconds!

Do You Remember?

Read each sentence below. Write *T* if the sentence is true. Write *F* if the sentence is false.

_____ **1.** Phineas Fogg was a real person.

_____ **2.** Nellie Bly was a reporter for the *World*.

_____ **3.** Nellie sailed from Italy to Asia on the *Victoria*.

_____ **4.** Sailors wanted Nellie to throw her monkey overboard.

_____ **5.** Nellie Bly beat Phineas Fogg's record.

Around the World (p. 3)

Critical Thinking — Fact or Opinion?

Write *F* before each statement that is a fact. Write *0* before each statement that is an opinion.

_____ **1.** It was foolish of Nellie to buy a monkey.

_____ **2.** Nellie got seasick on the way to England.

_____ **3.** Nellie Bly crossed the finish line on January 25, 1890.

_____ **4.** Jules Chambers should have gone with Nellie.

_____ **5.** Some people wrote songs about Nellie Bly.

Exploring Words

Use the words in the box to complete the paragraphs. Reread the paragraphs to be sure they make sense.

boasted	failure	editor	reporter
overboard	imaginary	seasick	informed

Nellie Bly was a **(1)** _____ for the *World*. Her

(2) _____ was Jules Chambers. In 1889 Chambers

asked Nellie to travel around the world. Nellie **(3)** _____ that she could

make the trip in 75 days and beat Phineas Fogg's **(4)** _____ record.

The trip to England was very rough. Nellie and the other passengers

became **(5)** _____. Two men were even washed **(6)** _____.

Meanwhile, back in New York, Chambers kept readers **(7)** _____ about

Nellie's trip. Nellie worried that she would not make it back in time. Then she

would feel like a **(8)** _____. Luckily, she was able to get back to

New York in just 72 days.

Joy Adamson

Joy Adamson hurried out of her tent in northern Kenya, a country in Africa. She ran over to the car where her husband, George, was waiting for her.

George pointed to the back of the car. There lay three tiny lion cubs. They were hiding their faces between their paws in fear. Joy's heart filled with love when she saw them. Carefully she scooped all three into her arms.

"The mother attacked me," George told Joy sadly. As a game warden, he often faced angry wild animals. "I had to shoot her. But I couldn't leave the babies to die."

Joy nodded. "They were only a few days old," she later wrote. "Their eyes were still covered with a bluish film. They could hardly crawl. How could I resist them?"

After a few days, the cubs had become part of the family. Each one had its own personality. Big One was the largest and quietest of the three. Lustica loved to clown around. And Elsa, the littlest and the weakest, was the most curious.

But, by July 1956, Joy knew something had to be done. The cubs were growing bigger and stronger every day. Their teeth and claws were becoming dangerously sharp. Sadly, she and George sent two of them to a zoo in Holland. Elsa was still the weakest. Joy decided to keep her until she was fully grown.

Elsa missed her sisters. But she soon learned to play by herself. Elsa loved her life with the Adamsons. When Joy or George went for a ride, Elsa went, too. She lay on the roof of the truck as it bounced along. Joy often took Elsa out into the bush. Elsa learned to chase zebras, giraffes, and buffalo. Most lions kill these animals for food. But Elsa didn't know how to kill. She had no mother to teach her.

Elsa wasn't worried about finding food. She trusted Joy to feed her and keep her safe. She often climbed into Joy's bed. She even let Joy pull out a tooth that was loose.

Joy loved Elsa's gentle ways. But she knew that soon even gentle Elsa would have to go to a zoo. Elsa was 23 months old. She was almost fully grown.

Elsa, however, had other ideas. In January 1958, she suddenly ran off into the bush. At dark, she refused to return. They called desperately for Elsa. No familiar sound came in answer. But presently they heard a chorus of lions a few hundred yards away.

53

Joy Adamson (p. 2)

After five hours, Elsa finally came back. She was tired and thirsty. Joy and George knew she had been out running with wild lions.

Suddenly, Joy was not sure Elsa belonged in a zoo. Perhaps she could be returned to the wild. Tame lions did not know how to hunt. They carried a human scent which made other lions stay away from them. But perhaps Elsa was smart enough to learn hunting skills. And perhaps she could win the trust of wild lions. With a mixture of hope and fear, the Adamsons decided to set Elsa free.

First, the Adamsons had to teach Elsa how to kill. George shot a small animal and let her eat it. In this way, she learned that dead animals could serve as food. The Adamsons also took Elsa to a spot where wild lions had killed a zebra. By watching them, Elsa learned how other lions ate.

At last the Adamsons decided to give Elsa a test. They drove her far from camp and set her free. After a few days they returned. Poor Elsa was very glad to see them. Clearly she didn't understand why they had gone away. And clearly she had eaten nothing since they left.

George taught Elsa more about killing. Elsa also learned how to make friends with other lions.

One day in 1959, a handsome male lion called to her. Elsa went charging off with him. Over the next few days, she made a few trips back to the Adamson's camp. And when she did come her stomach was full. Joy and George were thrilled. Elsa was killing her own food! And she had found a mate. It was hard for Joy to say goodbye to Elsa. But she knew that Elsa was happy and healthy. And most importantly, Elsa was where she belonged, living free with other lions.

Critical Thinking — Finding the Sequence

Number the sentences to show the order in which things happened in the story.

_____ The cubs became part of the family.

_____ The Adamsons set Elsa free.

_____ George brought home three lion cubs.

_____ Elsa went running with wild lions for the first time.

_____ Big One and Lustica were sent to a zoo.

Joy Adamson (p. 3)

Do You Remember?

In the blank, write the letter of the best ending for each sentence.

_____ **1.** Elsa's mother was killed by
    ⓐ hunters.   ⓑ wild elephants.   ⓒ George.

_____ **2.** Of the three cubs, Elsa was the
    ⓐ quietest.   ⓑ most curious.   ⓒ largest.

_____ **3.** George taught Elsa how to
    ⓐ kill for food.   ⓑ run.   ⓒ live in a cage.

_____ **4.** Elsa finally found
    ⓐ her mother and father.   ⓑ her sisters.   ⓒ a mate.

Exploring Words 🔍

Write the correct word in each sentence.

resist	personality	familiar	presently	chorus	film

1. A group of people or animals speaking or crying out at the same time is a _____.

2. A thin covering is a _____.

3. When you know something well, it is _____ to you.

4. Something that will happen soon will happen _____.

5. The things that make you different from others make up your _____.

6. When you try to keep from enjoying or liking something, you _____ it.

Tracking Bigfoot

Ellis Wright stopped dead in his tracks. He couldn't believe it. But there they were. They looked like 13 human footprints, only much larger. Wright stared at the prints in wonder. Who made them? And why were they here in a desert in New Mexico?

Wright put together a research team. He acted as the guide. The team studied each footprint. The prints seemed to have come from some giant human. But when were they made? And, more importantly, who or what made them?

Wright found the footprints in 1931. Since that time, they have been studied many times. Everyone agrees the prints were made by a living creature. But what kind of creature is it? Some people think they were made by camels more than 10,000 years ago. Still others think they were made by some huge two-legged creature. They call the creature "Bigfoot."

Bigfoot goes by many names. In Asia, he is called Yeti (YET ee). American Indians call him Sasquatch (SAS kwach). Others call him the Abominable Snowman. Whatever his name, he leaves his footprints all over the world. People have found them in Asia and North America.

But that still leaves a mystery. Is there really such a creature as Bigfoot? Why has no one ever found the body of a Bigfoot? And how could such a huge creature stay so well hidden? Maybe Bigfoot is just a fairy tale. But what about all the footprints? How do we explain them away? Could they all be fakes?

There is much more to the story of Bigfoot than just footprints. Over 1,000 people claim to have seen him.

Grover Krantz is one scientist who believes in Bigfoot. He talked to 36 of the people who have seen the creature. Krantz said, "I think that about half were lying. They were fooled by something else. With the other half, however, I couldn't find anything wrong."

What have these people seen? They describe a creature that is between seven and eight feet tall. He weighs about 800 pounds. He is covered with thick brown or black hair. He has less hair on his face, making him look a bit like a gorilla. Yet, Bigfoot doesn't walk like a gorilla. He walks on two legs like a human.

In October 1967, a man named

Tracking Bigfoot (p. 2)

Roger Patterson went looking for Bigfoot. He set up camp at Bluff Creek, California. Bigfoot's prints had been found in the area. Every day Patterson went out on his horse. He took a movie camera with him. One day he got lucky. Just as he rounded a bend, he saw something. It looked like a huge, black animal. Patterson's horse reared, tossing him to the ground.

Patterson scrambled to his feet. He ran back to the horse. The camera was still inside his saddlebag. At  last he got the camera ready. But by then, the creature was walking away. Patterson dashed after it. When he was about 80 feet away from it, he stopped and filmed Bigfoot disappearing into the bushes.

Patterson rushed to get the film developed. The pictures were fuzzy. But they showed a hairy creature about seven feet tall. The creature walked like a human. Was it a human dressed in a gorilla suit? Some people believe it was. Others, however, believe it really was Bigfoot. So the film didn't really solve anything. It just made the story of Bigfoot even more mysterious.

Do You Remember?

In the blank, write the letter of the best ending for each sentence.

_____ **1.** Wright showed people footprints he had found in the
ⓐ snow.   ⓑ desert.   ⓒ tar.

_____ **2.** Some people call Bigfoot
ⓐ Krantz.   ⓑ the Snow Angel.   ⓒ Sasquatch.

_____ **3.** Bigfoot is said to be
ⓐ 3 feet tall.   ⓑ 7 feet tall.   ⓒ 20 feet tall.

_____ **4.** Roger Patterson hoped to find
ⓐ Bigfoot.   ⓑ gold.   ⓒ his mother.

_____ **5.** Patterson was able to
ⓐ capture Bigfoot.   ⓑ film Bigfoot.   ⓒ talk with Bigfoot.

Tracking Bigfoot (p. 3)

Express Yourself

Imagine you are a newspaper reporter. You are about to interview Roger Patterson. On a separate piece of paper, write three questions that you would like to ask him.

Exploring Words

Choose the correct word from the box to complete each sentence.

mysterious	gorilla	claim	abominable	reared
research	filmed	fakes	scrambled	described

1. To study something carefully is to _____ it.

2. Things that are not real are _____.

3. Something that is horrible and hateful is _____.

4. If you have taken movie pictures of something, you have _____ it.

5. Something that is hard to understand is _____.

6. A horse that has kicked up its front legs is said to have _____ .

7. The largest ape that lives in the jungle is the _____.

8. When you have moved quickly on hands and knees, you have _____.

9. To state something as a fact is to make a _____.

10. When you have told about something in detail, you have _____ it.

A Monster in the Lake

The first time Alex Campbell saw the Loch Ness monster, he couldn't believe his eyes.

"It was May 1934. I was looking across the water. There was a great splash about 200 to 250 yards away. This huge neck appeared, stretching at least six feet above the water. It had a small head that kept turning nervously.

"I said to myself, 'This is fantastic.' Then I blinked my eyes. I just wanted to make sure it wasn't my imagination. But it was there, all right. Then a boat appeared. The creature saw it and, swoosh, what a dive!"

Since then, Alex Campbell has seen the creature 17 times. And more than 3,000 other sightings have been reported since the early 1930s.

Hopes of seeing the monster have brought many visitors to Loch Ness, a lake in northern Scotland. The deep lake is long and narrow. Its waters are often murky.

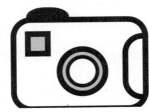

Tim Dinsdale wanted to prove that Nessie, as the monster is often called, was real. In 1960, he went to Loch Ness. He hoped to film Nessie.

Dinsdale camped by the shore. For the next six days, nothing happened. But then something caught his eye. Far out in the lake, he saw an object lying on the surface of the water.

The object started to move. Dinsdale turned on his movie camera. The creature turned left and then right and back to the left again. The strange thing moved up and down in the water. Finally, it disappeared for good.

Dinsdale rushed to have the film developed. The pictures weren't clear. But they showed a living thing moving in the water. It looked like Nessie. It fit the description other people had given. It had a long neck, a hump on its back, and was dark in color. Dinsdale was delighted.

In 1972, Robert Rines and a group of scientists went to Loch Ness. Like Dinsdale, Rines wanted to find out if the Loch Ness monster really existed. He took underwater cameras with lights. He also took sonar. Sonar sends out sound waves. These waves find objects underwater. Rines hoped these tools would help him take clear pictures of Nessie.

Rines and his workers went to the spot where Nessie had been seen most often. One morning the sonar screen showed a lot of fish quickly leaving the area. Then it picked up a large object. They photographed the large object.

The water in the lake is murky. So

A Monster in the Lake (p. 2)

once again, the pictures were not very good. But one of the pictures showed a creature with a long neck and flippers. That picture proved to some people that there was a large creature in Loch Ness. Others felt the pictures proved nothing.

More pictures were taken in 1975. This time scientists took several pictures that showed some kind of large, living body. It looked like a dragon. It measured about 20 feet with a long neck and a small head. One of the pictures showed the creature's head and open mouth facing the camera. But was it Nessie? No one could be sure.

And so the search and the sightings go on. Does the Loch Ness monster really exist? There is no clear proof one way or the other. The lake is more than 900 feet deep. Some people think that Nessie can hide in the deep water without being found. Maybe Nessie is very shy. Or maybe it shows itself only to those people who want to believe.

Do You Remember?

In the blank, write the letter of the best ending for each sentence.

_____ **1.** Loch Ness is a lake in
   ⓐ the United States.   ⓑ Canada.   ⓒ Scotland.

_____ **2.** People who claim to have seen Nessie say it has
   ⓐ no neck.   ⓑ two necks.   ⓒ a long neck.

_____ **3.** Tim Dinsdale believed Nessie was
   ⓐ a joke.   ⓑ real.   ⓒ dead.

_____ **4.** Robert Rines tried to find Nessie by using
   ⓐ airplanes.   ⓑ food.   ⓒ sonar.

A Monster in the Lake (p. 3)

Critical Thinking — Main Ideas

Underline the two most important ideas from the story.

1. There was a splash about 200 yards from Alex Campbell.

2. Many people claim to have seen the Loch Ness monster.

3. Scientists have been unable to prove whether or not Nessie is real.

4. The lake is more than 900 feet deep.

Exploring Words 🔍

Use the words in the box to complete the paragraphs. Reread the paragraphs to be sure they make sense.

sonar	imagination	fantastic	
hump	murky	existed	monster

Many people claim that a **(1)** _____ lives in the deep, **(2)** _____ waters of Loch Ness. These people all say it has a long neck and a large **(3)** _____ on its back. They have given it the nickname "Nessie."

Tim Dinsdale wanted to prove that Nessie really **(4)** _____. He waited by the lake for six days. Finally, he managed to take a picture. Scientists wondered if Nessie was just part of people's **(5)** _____. They went to Loch Ness and ran tests using **(6)** _____ and other equipment. The scientists wanted hard proof. But some people do not need hard proof to believe in the **(7)** _____ creature.

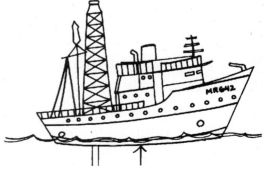

House of Terror

George Lutz awoke suddenly. It was 3:15 A.M. on December 23, 1975. George felt the urge to go downstairs. He crept down the stairs of his new home at 112 Ocean Avenue in Amityville, New York.

When he reached the first floor, a shiver ran down his back. He stared at the 250-pound, solid-wood front door. It was wide open and hanging by one hinge. The doorknob was twisted out of place. Someone — or something — had forced its way through the door!

George made a quick check of the house. There was no one else in it except his wife and three young children. He looked outside. There was no sign of anyone. The damage was all on the inside of the door. George was sure all the doors and windows were locked when they went to bed. And who would have the strength to pull the door off its hinges?

Other strange things began to happen in the house. His wife, Kathy, smelled perfume coming from empty rooms. She and George both saw a rocking chair rock all by itself. George saw a man's face appear on the basement walls. And night after night, George awoke at 3:15 A.M. Lying in the darkness, he knew something was wrong.

The Lutz family knew their house had a bad history. A year earlier, 24-year-old Ronnie DeFeo had killed his family in this house. He later said he heard voices that told him to do it. George and Kathy Lutz knew the story, but they didn't believe in ghosts or haunted houses.

Still, George decided to find out more about the DeFeo case. He was startled when he saw a picture of Ronnie DeFeo. This was the face that had been appearing on the walls! Then George learned the time of the murders. They took place at 3:15 A.M. That was the time George had been waking up!

One night George and Kathy went to bed late. Suddenly, they woke up. Their room was icy cold. All the windows on the second floor were wide open. Wind was whipping through the house.

George and Kathy ran from room to room closing the windows. Afterwards, they looked at each other in fear. Who or what had opened the windows on this cold winter night?

The next night brought more terror. George and Kathy glanced out their living room window. They saw a pair of red eyes staring at them. Running outside, they saw footprints in the snow. The footprints were like those of a pig. They led to the garage. When George and Kathy saw the garage door, they were too frightened to speak. The door had been pulled away from its metal frame. George and Kathy knew that no human being was strong enough to do such a thing. But that left them with a terrible question. If a human didn't do it, what did?

George and Kathy were not the only ones who sensed the presence of something or someone at 112 Ocean Avenue. A friend of theirs also noticed it. He said he heard a strange voice whisper to him to get out as he entered the house. After that, he could not think about the house without becoming sick. He refused to set foot in it again.

Kathy's aunt came to visit right after Christmas. But after only half an hour, she decided to leave. She said she had a bad feeling about the house.

As the days went by, there were more strange happenings. Green slime dripped from the ceiling. Kathy awoke with strange burn marks all over her stomach. Then five-year-old Missy said that a pig was coming into her room and talking to her at night. The boys saw a monster with no face in their room. Kathy and George strongly sensed something lurking in the house.

After 28 days, the family left the house in terror. They never returned — not even to get their furniture. They moved to California. There, they felt peace returning.

George and Kathy believe that they would have been harmed if they had stayed in the house. "These forces *are* real," said George. "And they do inflict evil whenever they get the chance."

What really happened at Amityville? Was the Lutz family trying to trick people? If so, why? Is it possible they were all dreaming the same bad dream? Or was the house truly haunted?

Critical Thinking - Main Ideas ⚡

Underline the most important idea from the story.

1. Ronnie DeFeo was 24 years old.

2. Many strange and frightening things happened in the Lutz house.

3. The address of the house was 112 Ocean Avenue.

House of Terror (p. 3)

Do You Remember?

In the blank, write the letter of the best ending for each sentence.

_____ **1.** George Lutz saw a face on the basement walls that looked like
ⓐ Ronnie DeFeo.   ⓑ Kathy Lutz.   ⓒ Kathy's aunt.

_____ **2.** A friend of the Lutz family became sick whenever he thought about the
ⓐ police.   ⓑ house.   ⓒ weather.

_____ **3.** One morning, Kathy's stomach was covered with
ⓐ burn marks.   ⓑ snow.   ⓒ spots.

_____ **4.** Missy Lutz said her room was visited at night by a
ⓐ ghost.   ⓑ baby.   ⓒ pig.

Exploring Words

Choose the correct word from the box to complete each sentence.

lurking	murder	solid	presence
evil	inflict	urge	haunted

1. A strong need to do something is an _____.

2. A house that is lived in by a ghost is said to be _____.

3. Someone who is hiding or sneaking about is _____.

4. If something is not hollow, it is _____.

5. Something that is bad and causes harm
is _____.

6. If you sense that someone is nearby, you sense
a _____.

7. To kill someone on purpose is to commit _____.

8. To do something harmful to someone is to _____ pain.

© Steck-Vaughn Company

Stories of Mystery
Nonfiction 4, SV 6179-6

No Lock Could Hold Him

The police officer walked into the locksmith's shop. He brought with him a handcuffed prisoner.

"The lock on these cuffs is broken," the police officer said. "I need you to cut the cuffs off."

Erich Weiss tried to cut the cuffs, but the steel was too hard. Weiss later said, "I broke six saw blades. Then a thought struck me. Maybe I could pick the lock."

Weiss succeeded. In fact, he picked the lock so easily that he soon tried others. Weiss used his new skill to put together a magic act. And he gave himself a new name — Harry Houdini.

Between 1895 and 1926, Houdini's act stunned the world. It seemed that he could escape from anything. He escaped from boxes, safes, and prison rooms.

In 1903, Houdini took his act to Russia. There he met Moscow's chief of police.

"Please lock me in your jail. I'd like to prove that I can escape from it," he said.

The chief had heard about Houdini's magic. He wanted no part in it. He turned Houdini down.

"How about the Carette, then?" Houdini asked.

The chief smiled. The Carette was a six-foot-square steel box. It was used to carry Russia's worst prisoners to Siberia. The Carette had two openings. One was a tiny window with bars. The other was a steel door. The chief could lock the door. But he could not unlock it. The key was 2,000 miles away in Siberia.

The chief made Houdini take off his clothes. He searched him for tools. He handcuffed Houdini and chained his legs together. Houdini got into the box, and the chief locked the door.

For the next 28 minutes, the chief waited. "He'll never get out," he thought.

But suddenly, Houdini appeared from behind the Carette. The door was still locked. The handcuffs and chains were also locked and lying on the floor. But somehow Houdini had escaped. No one ever found out how he did it.

Back in America, Houdini came up with another great act. A large glass box was placed on the stage. Houdini stood inside the box. A heavy piece of

Stories of Escape
Nonfiction 4, SV 6179-6

No Lock Could Hold Him (p. 2)

glass was lowered onto the box. The cover was locked on each side. Four tight straps passed over and under the box. Then water was poured into the box from a small hole in the top. Houdini was trapped. He had no way to reach the locks or straps. He had no way to breathe, either.

Houdini's helper pulled a curtain in front of the box. No one could breathe underwater. In four or five minutes he would drown. As the minutes passed, people began to panic. They feared Houdini was dead.

Then, suddenly, the curtain was pulled back. There stood Houdini, dripping wet. Behind him was the glass box. It was still filled with water. Its locks and straps were still in place. Houdini smiled at the people in the crowd. He had tricked them again.

Then Houdini came up with yet another trick. This time he climbed into a box that was bolted shut. The box was lowered six feet into the ground. The hole was filled with 3,000 pounds of sand.

The audience watched fearfully. Houdini was buried alive! He could never escape from the bolted box. And even if he did, he would be crushed by the heavy sand.

But all at once, the sand moved. A moment later, Houdini's curly head popped out. Once again the great Houdini had mysteriously escaped death.

Express Yourself ✒

Imagine that you are a reporter for a magazine. You have just seen Houdini escape from the glass box. On a separate piece of paper, write an article about what you saw.

No Lock Could Hold Him (p. 3)

Do You Remember?

In the blank, write the letter of the best ending for each sentence.

_____ 1. Before opening his magic act, Houdini worked in a
     ⓐ locksmith shop.   ⓑ post office.   ⓒ circus.

_____ 2. Houdini was the first person ever to escape from
     ⓐ Russia.   ⓑ the Carette.   ⓒ jail.

_____ 3. When Houdini came out of the glass box, he was
     ⓐ soaking wet.   ⓑ coughing.   ⓒ sick.

_____ 4. Houdini found it easy to
     ⓐ write books.   ⓑ bend coins.   ⓒ pick locks.

Exploring Words

Read each sentence. Fill in the circle next to the best meaning for the word in dark print. If you need help, use a dictionary.

1. Houdini **succeeded** in getting out of the Carette.
     ⓐ was able to   ⓑ feared   ⓒ forgot

2. People were **stunned** by Houdini's act.
     ⓐ angered   ⓑ badly hurt   ⓒ surprised

3. Houdini knew it was important not to **panic**.
     ⓐ become frightened ⓑ cry   ⓒ shout loudly

4. The box was **bolted** before it was put in the ground.
     ⓐ painted   ⓑ opened   ⓒ locked with a bar

5. The **audience** was afraid Houdini would drown.
     ⓐ child   ⓑ people watching ⓒ deaf person

6. People stared **fearfully** at the glass box.
     ⓐ with great hope   ⓑ with fear   ⓒ secretly

Name _____   Date _____

Alone on a Raft

It was World War II. The German submarine waited for just the right target. On the morning of November 23, 1942, it sighted a British ship. The submarine fired a torpedo at the ship.

The ship sank quickly. Fifty-four of the 55 people on board died. Only one person survived. He was 25-year-old Poon Lim. Although he had lived through the blast, Poon Lim was in serious trouble. He was alone, swimming helplessly in the middle of the Atlantic Ocean.

Luckily, one of the ship's rafts floated by. Poon Lim grabbed it and climbed on. He looked around for his shipmates. All he saw was water. Poon Lim's raft measured only six feet long by six feet wide. It had two containers on board. One held fresh water. The other contained chocolate, sugar, biscuits, fish paste, and a bottle of lime juice. There were also some flares that could be used to signal nearby ships.

Poon Lim looked carefully at the food he had. He decided to eat only six biscuits a day. Somehow he had to get more food. But how could he fish without a line or hook or bait?

As a child, Poon Lim had spent much time fishing. It was a good thing, for now he needed all his fishing skills. He had a piece of rope.

But it was much too thick to use as a fishing line. So Poon Lim pulled out some of the threads. Then he took a pin that held one of the flares together and made a fish hook.

Finding bait was harder. Poon Lim made a paste from biscuit powder. But it just washed off the hook. Then he found some barnacles under the raft. He picked the meat out of the tough shells. Poon Lim dropped his line over the side of the raft. After a while, he caught a fish.

"Little fish," he cried, "you have saved my life!"

Next Poon Lim caught a baby shark. He used its blood to attract other fish. Before long, he was able to scoop several small fish onto the raft. He didn't want to eat them all at once. So he tied rope to four posts on the raft. Then he hung the fish to dry.

After seven days on the raft, Poon Lim saw something in the distance. "It's a ship," he shouted. "I'm saved!"

Poon Lim fired his flares. But no one saw the tiny raft. "It was my

© Steck-Vaughn Company

Alone on a Raft (p. 2)

darkest day," Poon Lim said later.

But he didn't give up. He continued to fish. He found a way to collect fresh water. He sang songs to cheer himself up.

After about 100 days on the raft, his luck turned bad. The fish stopped biting. Over the next few days, he ate all the fish he had stored. Then he went five days without food. At last, some birds landed on the raft. Poon Lim waited until dark. Then, while the birds slept, he caught 13 of them and tied them up.

"Now, at least, I'll eat," he thought to himself.

Poon Lim continued to drift for many more days. Then he noticed something strange. The water had changed color. It was more brown than before. That could mean only one thing. He was near land!

On April 5, 1943, a fishing boat from Brazil rescued him. Poon Lim had drifted halfway across the Atlantic Ocean. He had survived 133 days at sea in an open raft — longer than any other person on record.

Do You Remember?

In the blank, write the letter of the best ending for each sentence.

_____ **1.** As a child, Poon Lim did a lot of

    ⓐ flying.   ⓑ fishing.   ⓒ fighting.

_____ **2.** Poon Lim used barnacles to

    ⓐ keep warm.   ⓑ catch fish.   ⓒ make biscuits.

_____ **3.** To stay cheerful, Poon Lim

    ⓐ sang songs.   ⓑ made flags.   ⓒ played games.

_____ **4.** On his raft, Poon Lim found some

    ⓐ guns.   ⓑ flares.   ⓒ books.

_____ **5.** Poon Lim was rescued by a

    ⓐ helicopter.   ⓑ submarine.   ⓒ fishing boat.

© Steck-Vaughn Company

Alone on a Raft (p. 3)

Critical Thinking — Finding the Sequence

Number the sentences to show the order in which things happened in the story.

_____ Poon Lim noticed that the water was changing color.

_____ Poon Lim caught 13 birds.

_____ Poon Lim tried to get the attention of a ship he saw in the distance.

_____ Poon Lim climbed onto the raft.

Exploring Words

Choose the correct word from the box to complete each sentence.

submarine	torpedo	shark
survive	barnacles	attract

1. A _____ is a ship that can travel underwater.

2. To _____ means to live through something dangerous.

3. _____ are small sea animals with hard shells.

4. A bomb that travels underwater is called a _____.

5. To _____ something means to bring it near.

6. A _____ is a dangerous fish with tough skin and rows of sharp teeth.

Crash Landing!

Spence Black and his wife, Beth, walked onto the Fort Worth airfield. They climbed into their small private airplane and took off. It was 9:00 P.M. on May 14, 1960.

Spence was an experienced pilot and was at the controls. But then, all at once, Spence let go of the controls and grabbed his chest. He slumped forward in his seat. Beth screamed out Spence's name, but he didn't answer. He was having a heart attack.

Panic washed over Beth. She reached across her husband's body and grabbed the wheel. She managed to steady the plane. Beth didn't know that she could have changed the controls over to her side.

With her free hand, she picked up the radio microphone.

"Help me! Won't somebody please help me!" she screamed.

No one answered her. When she looked back at Spence, she could tell he was dying. Tears ran down Beth's face. She didn't think she could go on without him. She wanted to die, too.

But then she thought of her five children. How could she leave them without a father or a mother? Beth knew what she had to do. She had to be there for her children. That meant she had to land the plane safely. She wiped her eyes and took a deep breath. She began looking for the lights of Dallas Love Field Airport. She also began sending new radio messages.

"SOS, Love Field! I'm in trouble, terrible trouble. Please help me!"

A controller at Love Field, Donald Potter, heard her call for help. He tried to reach her by radio. But Beth kept switching channels. Potter ordered all other planes off the runways. He told firefighters and crash trucks to stand by. And he watched for her approach.

As Beth Black reached Love Field, she saw a string of lights. She thought it was the runway, and she pointed the plane toward it. But it wasn't the runway. She was heading right for a highway!

Donald Potter saw what was happening. "Pull up, pull up!" he cried into his radio.

At last, Beth heard his warning. At the same time she saw the traffic on the highway. She pulled back on the wheel just in time.

Potter had to get her back to Love Field. "Turn around! Turn around!" he told her.

© Steck-Vaughn Company

Stories of Escape
Nonfiction 4, SV 6179-6

Crash Landing! (p. 2)

Beth swung the plane around. She flew back toward the airport. When she saw runway 31, she pushed the steering wheel forward. Again the plane dropped lower in the sky.

As the plane came down, it was shaking madly. Beth could see that the plane was moving too fast for a safe landing. But she didn't know how to slow down. She heard Donald Potter talking to her over the radio. But she couldn't understand what he was telling her.

Then, a few seconds before landing, she remembered something. Spence always pushed a couple of buttons before landing. She found a button marked "flaps." She pushed it, and instantly the plane slowed down. Then she pushed a second button marked "landing gear."

The plane was still going too fast to land. In a last desperate move, she shut off the engine. Then, stretched out across Spence, she fainted.

Donald Potter and others watched in fear as the plane hit the runway. It bounced 40 feet into the air. Then it landed again about 300 yards away. The engine snapped off in the crash. The wings and body were crushed.

Rescue workers found Beth Black sitting on one of the crushed airplane wings. Her left arm was broken, and her jaw was cracked. But she was alive. Spence Black had died before the plane ever landed. The heart attack had killed him.

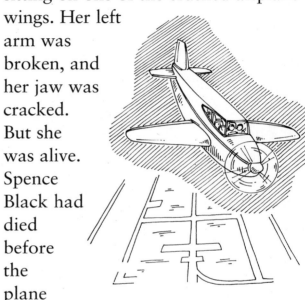

Later, Beth Black talked about her escape from death. "By rights, I should have been killed in the crash at Love Field, but I wasn't. Now it's my job to make the most of this wonderful gift of life."

Express Yourself ✎

Pretend you are a newspaper reporter. On a separate piece of paper, write a story telling about Beth Black's experience. Tell who, what, when, where, and why.

Crash Landing! (p. 3)

Do You Remember?

Read each sentence below. Write **T** if the sentence is true. Write **F** if the sentence is false.

_____ **1.** Beth Black had never landed an airplane.

_____ **2.** Spence died of a heart attack.

_____ **3.** Donald Potter thought Beth was joking when he got her radio message.

_____ **4.** Beth turned off the engine before the plane hit the ground.

_____ **5.** Beth walked away from the crash without any injuries.

Exploring Words

Use the words in the box to complete the paragraphs. Reread the paragraphs to be sure they make sense.

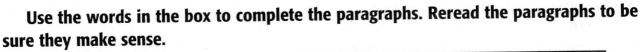

| runway | microphone | slumped | gear | controls |

Spence Black had a heart attack in his plane. He **(1)** _____

forward in his seat. His wife, Beth, picked up the radio **(2)** _____

and asked for help.

At last, she heard Donald Potter's voice. He helped

her find the airport and the **(3)** _____.

She figured out how to use some of the plane's

(4) _____. She lowered the landing

(5) _____. Beth was hurt, but she lived through the crash.

Fire! Fire! Fire!

Dennis Rogan went to bed early. He fell asleep quickly in the warm October air. Then suddenly he awoke. He heard shouting.

"Fire!" someone yelled.

Rogan jumped up and ran outside. The O'Learys' barn was on fire. Rogan ran next door to the O'Learys' house. He pounded on the door to warn them. Then he ran for safety. Later, he asked another neighbor how the fire started.

The neighbor said, "Mrs. O'Leary's cow kicked over a lantern. It landed in the hay, and now everything is on fire!"

No one knows if the cow really did knock over a lantern. But one thing is certain. At about 8:45 P.M. on October 8, 1871, fire broke out on the West Side of Chicago. The fire started in the O'Learys' barn. A nearby store owner spotted the fire. He rang a fire alarm. But the message never reached the fire station.

A lookout on the courthouse tower also spotted the flames. His alarm did reach the station. But he made a mistake. He thought the fire was coming from a different place. His alarm sent firefighters rushing in the wrong direction.

The bad luck didn't end there. When a fire truck finally arrived at the barn, it broke down. Firefighters could not fight the fire until they repaired the truck.

Lack of rain added to the problem. A drought had spread over the midwestern part of the U.S. Everything was dry and dusty and ready to burn. To make matters worse, a 25 mile-per-hour wind sent sparks flying from house to house.

The fire spread quickly. It ate through the wooden barn and leaped to other buildings. Homes and businesses went up in flames. Almost all of the buildings were made of wood. Sidewalks and fences were wooden, too. So there was nothing to slow the fire down. Thousands of people from the West Side had to leave their homes. They took what they could and ran for their lives.

By 9:30 P.M., several city blocks glowed red. The blaze roared up the West Side. At 11:30 P.M. it leaped across the Chicago River where people

Fire! Fire! Fire! (p. 2)

had thought they were safe. Suddenly, they too had to run for their lives.

Smoke filled the air. Huge tongues of flames dashed across the sky. "There were moments I could see buildings melt," one witness said. Another said, "It was a sea of fire. The air was filled with burning embers. The wind blew fiercely. Thousands upon thousands of people

rushed about, burned out of shelter and without food."

Finally, it began to rain. After 26 long hours, the firefighters were able to put out the fires. By that time, the city lay in ruins. Over 2,000 acres were destroyed. Property damage was $196 million. Over 100,000 people lost their homes. And about 300 people lost their lives.

Those who lived began to rebuild the city. They brought in famous builders to put up beautiful new buildings. This time they learned from their past experience. The buildings were made with stone and brick. Soon Chicago was once again a busy, lively city.

Do You Remember?

In the blank, write the letter of the best ending for each sentence.

_____ **1.** The fire leaped across
      ⓐ Lake Michigan. ⓑ the Chicago River. ⓒ Hudson Bay.

_____ **2.** The summer of 1871 was very
      ⓐ dry. ⓑ wet. ⓒ short.

_____ **3.** The first fire truck to get to the fire
      ⓐ caught fire. ⓑ broke down. ⓒ had no water.

_____ **4.** The fire was spread by the
      ⓐ wind. ⓑ river. ⓒ horse.

_____ **5.** Most sidewalks, fences, and buildings were made of
      ⓐ wood. ⓑ steel. ⓒ bricks.

Fire! Fire! Fire! (p. 3)

Critical Thinking — Drawing Conclusions

Finish each sentence by writing the best answer.

1. Dennis Rogan knocked on the O'Learys' door because _____

_____.

2. Firefighters rushed off in the wrong direction because_____

_____.

3. People ran out of their homes because _____

_____.

Exploring Words

Use the words in the box to complete the paragraphs. Reread the paragraphs to be sure they make sense.

lantern	embers	fiercely	fled	shingles	acres

On October 8, 1871, a fire began to burn **(1)** _____ on the West

Side of Chicago. No one knew how it started. Some people

said a cow kicked a **(2)** _____ into the hay.

Firefighters couldn't stop the blaze.

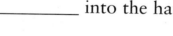

As the fire spread, people **(3)** _____ from their homes. They

saw **(4)** _____ from the fire flying through the air. They saw

(5) _____ torn from rooftops flying in the wind. By the time the fire

died, over 2,000 **(6)** _____ had been destroyed.

© Steck-Vaughn Company

Stories of Disaster
Nonfiction 4, SV 6179-6

A City Under Snow

On March 11, 1888, a freezing rain fell on New York City. Strong gusts of wind drove the rain sideways. By dawn on March 12, the rain had turned to snow. It fell from the sky as sharp, icy flakes. Winds of 80 miles per hour kept the snow swirling madly in the air. Snowdrifts reached 20 feet or more. Many New Yorkers did not realize how bad the storm was. Looking out their windows, they saw nothing but white, blowing snow. Still, they thought it would end soon. They thought it was just a small snowstorm.

In Harlem, Mrs. Charles Green bundled up her ten-year-old nephew, Sam Strong.

"There, you could go to the North Pole in that outfit," she said cheerfully. "Hurry now, so you won't be late for school."

Sam couldn't see a thing as he walked outside. The wind drove icy snow into his cheeks and down his neck. When he turned onto Lenox Avenue, the wind grabbed him and threw him into a deep snowdrift. The snow was way over his head. Sam tried to move his hands and feet. But he couldn't. Five minutes passed. Then ten. Then fifteen. Panic began to sweep over him. He feared he might die buried in the snow.

At last a police officer passed the snowdrift. He heard young Sam's cries. The officer clawed away at the snowdrift. Finally, he reached Sam and pulled him out.

"You shouldn't be out in this, Sonny," he said. "You go straight home."

It took Sam hours to get back home. His ears were stinging. His face hurt. He barely had enough energy to crawl through the drift to his front porch. But he was one of the lucky ones. The Blizzard of '88 caused nearly 100 people to die that day in New York City alone.

All over the city, things came to a sudden stop. Milk couldn't be delivered, so babies went hungry. Because coal deliveries stopped, families could not heat their homes. Street cars and cabs stopped running. Thousands of workers had no way to get home.

As the day went on, the city took on an eerie look. The wind flung boxes, signs, and benches down the street. Thousands of sparrows dropped from the sky. They had frozen. Horses, too, lay dead in the streets. Many were still tied to the wagons they had been pulling.

People staggered through the

© Steck-Vaughn Company

Stories of Disaster
Nonfiction 4, SV 6179-6

A City Under Snow (p. 2)

streets, looking for open grocery stores. The icy snow cut at their faces until they bled. At stores they bought gloves and shovels. They begged for food and coal.

Later, these people searched for words to describe the snow and wind. "It felt like lashes of a whip," said one person.

"The air was full of fine needles of snow," one man remembered. "The sleet striking my face made me feel as if it was raining carpet tacks. Little icicles formed on my eyelashes and got into my eyes. They felt like hot cinders."

By the third day, the blizzard started dying down. The wind dropped, and the snow stopped falling. That afternoon the sun poked through the clouds. Slowly, New York City came to life again.

The blizzard was over. But the memory of it stayed. The storm had destroyed homes all along the East Coast. It did $20 million worth of damage in New York City alone. It also took the lives of almost 300 people.

Those who lived never forgot it. Certainly Sam Strong never did. As long as he lived, he never forgot the force of the wind that March day. He never forgot the terror of being trapped in a huge mountain of snow. And he never forgot the kind police officer who saved his life.

Do You Remember?

Read each sentence below. Write _T_ if the sentence is true. Write _F_ if the sentence is false.

_____ **1.** Snowdrifts reached 20 feet.

_____ **2.** Sam Strong almost died in a river.

_____ **3.** Thousands of sparrows froze.

_____ **4.** The blizzard lasted less than 24 hours.

_____ **5.** People who lived through the blizzard never forgot it.

A City Under Snow (p. 3)

Express Yourself ✎

Pretend you are Sam Strong. You have just made it home after being saved by the police officer. On a separate piece of paper, write an entry in your journal telling about this day.

Exploring Words 🔍

Read each sentence. Fill in the circle next to the best meaning for the word in dark print. If you need help, use a dictionary.

1. People had no warning that a **blizzard** was coming.
   - ⓐ heavy snowstorm with high winds
   - ⓑ thunderstorm
   - ⓒ dust storm

2. Icy **flakes** cut people's faces.
   - ⓐ small bits of snow
   - ⓑ winds
   - ⓒ drops

3. The high winds kept the snow **swirling** in the air.
   - ⓐ hanging
   - ⓑ moving
   - ⓒ freezing

4. Sam had trouble getting through the deep **snowdrifts**.
   - ⓐ piles of snow
   - ⓑ snowstorms
   - ⓒ puddles

5. The dark streets looked **eerie**.
   - ⓐ strange
   - ⓑ quiet
   - ⓒ dangerous

6. The wind **flung** signs to the ground.
   - ⓐ flew
   - ⓑ stretched
   - ⓒ threw

7. During the first night, the rain turned to **sleet**.
   - ⓐ icy rain
   - ⓑ gentle mist
   - ⓒ soft snow

8. **Icicles** stuck to one man's eyelashes.
   - ⓐ drops of rain
   - ⓑ spikes of ice
   - ⓒ frost

A Mountain Erupts

David Johnston, a volcano expert, stared into his binoculars. There it was! He could see the lump on the side of the mountain. It was getting bigger. Any moment now it would erupt.

It was exactly 8:31 A.M. on May 18, 1980. Seconds later, Mount St. Helens exploded.

Johnston had wanted to get a good look at Mount St. Helens. So he climbed to a spot five miles away from the mountain. It wasn't far enough. He was never heard from again.

The experts knew that Mount St. Helens near Vancouver, Washington, would blow up. The only question was when. A small eruption took place on March 27, 1980. For the next eight weeks, the volcano steamed and rumbled. People everywhere followed the reports day by day.

The people who lived in the area were told to leave while they still could. Many people did not want to leave. George Pickett, a logger, lived with his family on nearby Toutle River. He and 200 other loggers were supposed to cut trees near the mountain on Monday, May 19.

Luckily, Pickett was at home Sunday morning. He heard a noise.

"There was a roar, like a jet plane approaching, and a lot of snapping and popping. Those were the trees. We got out fast."

The power of a volcano is hard to imagine. This one had 500 times the force of a bomb. The blast blew 1,200 feet off the top of the mountain. It shot ash 12 miles into the sky. The volcano also caused giant mud slides. These mud slides destroyed everything in their path.

David Crockett was a photographer for a TV station. He happened to be in the wrong place at the wrong time. He was on a dirt road at the bottom of Mount St. Helens. All of a sudden, he heard the blast. He looked up. He saw a huge wall of hot mud. It was rushing straight toward him.

Luckily, the river of mud split in two. It shot past him on both sides of the road. Ash filled the air. It was hard for him to breathe. All he could do was to keep walking down the road. He recorded what was happening.

"I am walking toward the only light I can see. I can hear the mountain rumble. At this very moment I have to say I believe I am dead. The ash burns my eyes! It's very, very hard to breathe and very dark. If I could only breathe air. I will try the radio. Mayday! Mayday! Ash is

A Mountain Erupts (p. 2)

coming down on me heavily. I want to live!"

Crockett made it out alive. A helicopter saved him. But by that time, he had spent ten long hours wondering if he would die.

The volcano killed 60 people. The mud slides wiped out 123 homes. They also destroyed bridges, roads, and wildlife. Over 150 square miles of trees were flattened. Lumber companies lost about $500 million. In nearby lakes and streams, fish died by the millions. The eruption turned the whole area into a wasteland.

The volcanic ash caused other problems. People 100 miles away could barely breathe. They had to wear masks over their mouths. Some towns had several inches of ash on the streets. One writer wrote, "Spokane looked like an ashtray."

But it could have been much worse. Luckily, not many people lived near Mount St. Helens. And this volcano was only average in size. Still, Mount St. Helens was large enough to remind us of how powerful nature is.

Do You Remember?

Read each sentence below. Write *T* if the sentence is true. Write *F* if the sentence is false.

_____ **1.** No one expected Mt. St. Helens to blow up.

_____ **2.** George Pickett and his family escaped from the volcano.

_____ **3.** Ash was shot 12 miles into the sky.

_____ **4.** David Crockett died in a boiling sea of mud.

_____ **5.** Ash filled the air and made it hard to breathe.

A Mountain Erupts (p. 3)

Express Yourself

Pretend you are David Crockett. You have just been rescued after spending ten hours trapped near the volcano. On a separate piece of paper, describe to your family what happened and how you feel.

Exploring Words

Use the clues to complete the puzzle. Choose from the words in the box.

volcano	binoculars
erupt	logger
photographer	helicopter
wasteland	mask
average	powerful

Across

2. a person who takes pictures
6. glasses used to see things far away
7. an exploding mountain
9. a cover used to protect the face
10. a person who cuts down trees

Down

1. to explode
3. aircraft without wings
4. strong
5. an empty or destroyed place
8. medium size

A Park in Flames

Scientists in Yellowstone Park expected the summer of 1988 to be an ordinary summer — cool and wet. But this would be the driest summer in 112 years.

Fires began easily in the dry weather. Some fires were started by lightning. Others were caused by careless people. The fires ate up leaves, logs, and pine needles. The flames gained strength as they moved. They destroyed everything in their paths.

"Why don't the park officials do something?" one woman cried. "Why don't they send out firefighters to stop the blazes?"

For over 100 years the National Park Service had fought all fires in Yellowstone as soon as they started. But scientists now felt that this was a mistake. They thought that fires were nature's way of cleaning out the forest.

In 1972, the Park Service began to fight fires started by humans. Fires started naturally would be allowed to burn. If natural fires threatened lives or property, they would be fought. When the fires in Yellowstone Park began in June 1988, park officials battled only some of the blazes. But the fires kept growing and growing.

People who lived in nearby towns complained. They feared the fires would drive away the tourists. "We'd see the fire get bigger and bigger. They wouldn't do a thing about it," said one motel owner.

On July 21, park officials declared war on all fires in the park. By then, the fires were huge. Nine thousand firefighters poured into Yellowstone. Some came in helicopters. They tried to fight the fire from the air. Others stayed on the ground. They came with bulldozers and chain saws. They hurried to clear wide strips of land. The workers hoped these strips would stop the fires.

Day after day, the firefighters battled the flames. But they could not put them out. The weather was just too dry and windy.

On September 9, the fires were still burning. Firefighters fought to save the park buildings. They sprayed the famous Old Faithful Inn with water and chemicals. The 200-foot wall of flames roared closer. The firefighters ran to safety. When the smoke cleared, they were glad to see that the hotel still stood. The large parking lot around it had saved it.

By mid-September, Yellowstone Park was completely closed to visitors. Many people thought officials had waited too long to begin fighting the fires.

© Steck-Vaughn Company

Stories of Disaster
Nonfiction 4, SV 6179-6

A Park in Flames (p. 2)

Others blamed the high winds and drought. Of the 13 big fires in Yellowstone, eight had been fought from the start. All eight were still burning. "Even with every weapon, men cannot always put out a wildfire," one official said.

As the fall weather set in, the fires did slow down. But they didn't die until the November snow came. It was nature itself that finally put out the blazes. By then, one fifth of the park had been burned.

Some people thought the fires were a disaster. They felt that park officials should have acted more quickly. But scientists did not agree.

"These fires are natural events," said scientist James Schmitt. Scientists thought that the fires might be good for the park. The flames burned the biggest, driest trees. That left room for new trees to grow.

Whether good or bad, the results of the summer of 1988 will be with us for many years.

Critical Thinking — Finding the Sequence

Number the sentences to show the order in which things happened in the story.

_____ Many firefighters came in to fight the fires.

_____ Fires were started by lightning and careless people.

_____ The fires died out when the winter snows came.

_____ Yellowstone officials declared war on the fires.

A Park in Flames (p. 3)

Do You Remember?

Read each sentence below. Write _T_ if the sentence is true. Write _F_ if the sentence is false.

1. _____ Some of the fires were started by lightning.

2. _____ Gusts of wind made the fires easier to control.

3. _____ Firefighters tried to stop the fires by clearing strips of land.

4. _____ Nine thousand firefighters could not put out the fires.

5. _____ The fires were finally put out by snow in November.

Exploring Words

Write the correct word in each sentence.

officials	threatened	weapon	events	naturally

1. _____ are things that happen.

2. People who are in charge of something are called _____.

3. To be put in danger is to be _____.

4. A _____ is something to fight with.

5. If something happens _____, it is caused by nature.

A Pirate's Last Stand

The people of North Carolina were terrified. At night they locked their houses. They prayed that they would be spared.

The cause of all this terror was one man — the pirate Blackbeard. No one dared to stand up to him. But among themselves, the people whispered, "Something must be done. Blackbeard takes whatever he wants from us. Soon we will all be ruined."

Blackbeard was known the world over for his long, black beard. He braided it and tied the ends with ribbons. He wrapped the braids around his ears. He was a huge man with wild eyes.

Throughout 1717 and 1718, Blackbeard sailed the Carolina coast. He traveled in a ship called _Queen Anne's Revenge_. Blackbeard would capture ships. He stole their cargo. Then he would kill the sailors or leave them to die on small islands.

Sometimes Blackbeard left the sea. He attacked North Carolina towns. He and his pirates robbed many homes. They would kill anyone who tried to stop them. The people of North Carolina asked their governor to protect them. But he had become friends with the pirate.

The people of North Carolina went to Governor Spotswood of Virginia. Spotswood agreed that Blackbeard had to be stopped. "I will send the Navy out after him," he said.

There was one man in the Navy who was not afraid of Blackbeard. That man was Robert Maynard. Governor Spotswood asked Maynard to lead a group of men against the pirate.

"Shall I take him dead or alive?" asked Maynard.

"I don't care," said Spotswood. "Just get rid of him."

Maynard and his crew set out at once. On November 17, 1718, he discovered Blackbeard's hiding place.

Maynard gathered his men together. "In the morning," he said, "we'll sail up the inlet and attack Blackbeard."

One of Maynard's men spoke up. "The _Queen Anne's Revenge_ has many cannons. We have no cannons. How can we hope to beat Blackbeard?"

"We will make a surprise attack," answered Maynard.

On November 22, Maynard and his men rowed toward the _Queen Anne's Revenge_. Suddenly a shot was

© Steck-Vaughn Company

A Pirate's Last Stand (p. 2)

fired from the pirate ship. Maynard raised his flag and continued toward the ship. Blackbeard demanded to know who they were.

"You see we are no pirates," answered Maynard.

Maynard's answer made Blackbeard angry. But Maynard showed no fear. The pirates fired at them. Many men were killed. Still Maynard didn't give up. He ordered all the men to go below except himself and the man steering. Then they sailed up close to the pirate ship.

When Blackbeard saw the empty ship, he laughed. "Come on," he said to his men. "Let's go finish them off!" Blackbeard and some of his pirates jumped onto Maynard's ship. At once, the rest of Maynard's men came up from below and attacked the pirates.

Blackbeard and Maynard saw each other. The two men fired their guns at the same time. Blackbeard missed. Maynard's bullet hit the pirate. But Blackbeard did not fall.

Blackbeard leaped at Maynard with his sword waving. With one blow, he cut the blade off Maynard's sword. Maynard's men cut the pirate with their swords. Still he didn't fall. They shot at him with their guns. Finally Blackbeard fell to the deck, dead. The few pirates who were left alive gave up.

"At last!" said Maynard. "The people of North Carolina can again live in peace."

People all along the coast celebrated. Sailors everywhere rejoiced. Robert Maynard had put an end to one of the cruelest pirates ever to sail the seas.

Critical Thinking — Finding the Sequence ⚡

Write *1* before the sentence that tells what happened first in the story. Write *2* before the sentence that tells what happened next, and so on.

_____ Maynard and his crew found Blackbeard's hiding place.

_____ Sailors everywhere rejoiced.

_____ Governor Spotswood asked Maynard to get rid of Blackbeard.

_____ Blackbeard jumped onto Maynard's ship.

Name_____   Date_____

A Pirate's Last Stand (p. 3)

Do You Remember?

In the blank, write the letter of the best ending for each sentence.

1. Blackbeard was known the world over for
   ⓐ his long, black beard.   ⓑ being kind.   ⓒ his good looks.

2. Maynard hated
   ⓐ Governor Spotswood.   ⓑ Queen Anne.   ⓒ pirates.

3. Maynard discovered Blackbeard's
   ⓐ gold.   ⓑ hiding place.   ⓒ secret log.

4. Maynard and his men had no
   ⓐ swords.   ⓑ cannons.   ⓒ food.

5. After Blackbeard fell, the pirates who were left alive
   ⓐ kept fighting.   ⓑ swam away.   ⓒ gave themselves up.

Exploring Words

Write the correct word in each sentence.

terrified	spared	pirate
governor	demanded	rejoiced

1. A sailor who robs other ships is a _____.

2. Something that has not been harmed has been _____.

3. If you _____, you felt glad about something.

4. To be very frightened is to be _____.

5. A _____ is the leader in charge of a state.

6. If you asked for something as though it was your right, you _____ it.

Voice for the Children

Florence Kelley stared in horror at the giant room full of furnaces. "So this is what a glass factory is like," she thought. The only light came from the flaming furnaces. In front of these furnaces, glass blowers sat working. Dozens of young boys hurried around. They carried heavy buckets of water or sat next to the furnaces, cleaning tools. The boys looked tired and dirty. They had cuts and burns from the hot glass.

"I can't believe it!" Florence thought angrily. "I can't believe young boys work in places like this!"

Florence Kelley was only 12 years old when she visited this glass factory. Her father took her there. He wanted to show her the wonders of new factories. He wanted her to see how quickly things were made. But Kelley also saw how awful the factory was for child workers. She could not forget the small boys crouching by the hot furnaces. "It was a picture I carried with me all my days," she later wrote.

Later, Kelley learned that over one million children worked in factories. They were hot, crowded, and unsafe. Many children worked 12 hours a day, six or seven days a week. Factory owners didn't have to pay children as much as older workers. Every year tens of thousands of child workers were hurt or killed. In some factories, children handled pots of acid or boiling water. Often they were badly burned. Some children ran large machines. Some of these children lost fingers, arms, or legs. Most factories had no fresh air. There was no protection from dirt and disease. Many factory owners locked their doors. If a fire broke out, the workers inside could not escape. Many child workers died.

"Something must be done!" said Kelley. In 1889, she wrote a paper. She told of the horrors children faced in factories. She asked all Americans to help change things. "Do not buy goods made by child workers!" she cried. "Buy from companies that don't hire children!"

Kelley also asked the government to help. She wanted new laws. She wanted a law keeping all children under 16 years old in school. Kelley spoke to anyone who would listen. In a few years, she was famous. Everyone knew her as a leader in the fight against child labor.

In 1893, Florence Kelley fought for a new law. The law said factory owners could not hire young children.

© Steck-Vaughn Company

Stories of Heroes
Nonfiction 4, SV 6179-6

Voice for the Children (p. 2)

The law also created a Chief Factory Inspector to make sure factories were following the new law.

The Governor of Illinois asked her to be the Chief Factory Inspector. Kelley's first months as Inspector were not easy. Day after day she traveled to dark, dirty factories. She ordered the factory owners to stop using young workers. Owners hated to see Kelley coming. Many were rude to her. One took out his gun. He fired a couple of warning shots.

He thought it would scare her off. But he was wrong. Kelley's life was in danger. But she would not stop her work. She cared more about the safety of children than she did about her own safety.

Then smallpox broke out. Many people died. It was easily passed from one person to another. It could even be passed on in clothing. The best way to stop smallpox was to keep the sick people away from everyone else. Clothing made by sick people should also be kept away.

"Sick people are still sewing clothes," Kelley thought. "They are passing the disease on to all the child workers. And the clothes they make are sold in stores. People buy the clothes and carry smallpox home."

Kelley knew she had to act. She made sick workers stop working. She also got rid of the clothes they had made.

"Burn them!" she ordered owners. Thousands of dollars worth of clothing were burned.

Factory owners were very angry. Still, Kelley did not back down.

When Florence Kelley's time as Inspector was over, there was still much to be done. Yet Kelley had started to change the way people think. People began to see that it was wrong to use child workers. Florence Kelley never gave up the fight to protect America's children.

Critical Thinking — Drawing Conclusions

Finish each sentence by writing the best answer.

1. Many child workers lost their lives in factory fires because _____.

2. Factory owners hated to see Kelley coming because _____.

Voice for the Children (p. 3)

Do You Remember?

In the blank, write the letter of the best ending for each sentence.

_____ **1.** When Florence Kelley was 12 years old, she saw boys working in a
       ⓐ circus.   ⓑ school.   ⓒ factory.

_____ **2.** Kelley thought children should
       ⓐ go to church.   ⓑ be in school.   ⓒ work part time.

_____ **3.** One factory owner tried to scare Kelley away with a
       ⓐ gun.   ⓑ dog.   ⓒ car.

_____ **4.** Smallpox could be carried by
       ⓐ books.   ⓑ clothing.   ⓒ glass.

_____ **5.** Kelley made factory owners burn thousands of dollars worth of
       ⓐ hay.   ⓑ food.   ⓒ clothes.

Exploring Words

Find the best meaning for the word in dark print. Fill in the circle next to it.

1. Florence Kelley felt **horror** when she saw the glass factory.

       ⓐ fear and dislike   ⓑ joy   ⓒ cold

2. Kelley saw small boys **crouching** by the hot furnaces.

       ⓐ sleeping   ⓑ bending down   ⓒ eating

3. Some children handled pots of **acid**.

       ⓐ a chemical that can burn you   ⓑ soup   ⓒ water

4. Kelley worked against child **labor**.

       ⓐ schooling   ⓑ rights   ⓒ work

5. Some factory workers were **rude** to Kelley.

       ⓐ ready to help   ⓑ kind   ⓒ not polite

© Steck-Vaughn Company

Teacher with a Dream

Mrs. Patsy McLeod opened the door to her tiny cabin. "Come on," she called to eight-year-old Mary. "It is time to deliver the wash."

"Yes, Mama," said Mary. Together she and Mrs. McLeod carried the clean clothes to the house up the road. Mary, a poor African-American girl, liked going there. She enjoyed seeing the beautiful things inside. On this day, she picked up a book lying on the table. The daughter of the white owner grabbed it away from her. "Put that down," the girl snapped. "You can't read!"

It hurt Mary to know that the girl was right. On the way home, she looked up at her mother. "I want to learn to read," she said.

Two years later, a woman named Emma Wilson came to Mayesville. She set up a school for African-American children. Miss Wilson asked the McLeods if any of their children could attend. Mr. McLeod needed his 17 children to help pick cotton. He could only spare one worker. He decided Mary should be the one.

Mary did well at school. In the evenings, she taught her brothers and sisters to read. Mary also learned arithmetic. She went to the market with her father to make sure he wasn't cheated when he sold his cotton.

Mary graduated from Emma Wilson's school in 1888 at the age of 12. There was no nearby high school for African-American children. So she went back to the farm.

Again, however, help came her way. A woman named Mary Chrissman from Denver, Colorado, wanted to help. She offered to pay to send one African-American girl to high school. Emma Wilson gave Chrissman Mary's name.

With Chrissman's help, Mary spent seven years at Scotia Seminary in Concord, North Carolina. She took high school and college classes. She was an outstanding student. At night, she worked washing floors, baking bread, and waiting on tables. On June 13, 1894, she graduated.

"Miss Chrissman believed in me," she said to herself. "Now it's my turn to offer hope to others." For the next few years, Mary taught at several different schools. In 1898, she met and married Albertus Bethune.

In 1904, Mary moved to Florida. She wanted to open her own school. But she had just $1.50 in her pocket. Mary found an empty shack with seven small rooms. The rent was $11 a month. To raise the money, Mary baked sweet potato pies.

Mary found five girls whose parents could afford to pay 50 cents a week. Mary's own son was the sixth student.

Stories of Heroes

Teacher with a Dream (p. 2)

Mary had no supplies. So she made ink by squeezing juice from berries. She made pencils from burned wood. She used boxes for desks. She used peach baskets for seats. She begged for supplies door-to-door. She later said, "Many people gave me things just to get rid of me."

Mary opened her school on October 3, 1904. Mary's students quickly learned to read, write, and count. Other families wanted to send their children to Mary's school. Some were too poor to pay. Mary took them in anyway. She made them new clothes. She taught them to sew and cook for themselves. Soon even adults wanted to attend Mary's school. So Mary began teaching evening classes. In just two years, the school had four teachers and 250 students.

Mary needed more room. She wanted to buy land so she wouldn't have to pay rent. But she couldn't afford good land. She went to the owner of the town garbage dump and asked to buy it. The owner asked for $200. Mary paid $5 right away. She promised to pay the rest over the next two years. She and her students burned or carted off the garbage. Slowly they cleared the land.

Mary knew that they needed money. She called on everyone in town. She could talk almost anyone into helping her.

In 1907 Mary's dream came true. A new four-story school building stood on the old town dump. She named it Faith Hall. Over the door it said, "Enter to Learn." On the other side it said, "Depart to Serve." Mary McLeod Bethune continued to serve her students and educate others about the needs of African Americans until her death in 1955.

Do You Remember?

In the blank, write the letter of the best ending for each sentence.

_____ **1.** As a young girl, Mary wanted to
ⓐ become a dancer.   ⓑ learn to read.   ⓒ move to Africa.

_____ **2.** Mary raised money for her school by
ⓐ selling pies.   ⓑ training horses.   ⓒ working in a factory.

_____ **3.** Mary held evening classes for
ⓐ blind people.   ⓑ adults.   ⓒ whites.

_____ **4.** To get land for her school, Mary bought
ⓐ the town dump.   ⓑ a pond.   ⓒ an old train station.

© Steck-Vaughn Company

Stories of Heroes

Nonfiction 4, SV 6179-6

Name_____   Date_____

Teacher with a Dream (p. 3)

Critical Thinking — Fact or Opinion

Write **F** before each statement that is a fact. Write **0** before each statement that is an opinion.

_____ **1.** Mary's family was poor.

_____ **2.** A woman in Denver paid for Mary to attend Scotia Seminary.

_____ **3.** It was foolish of Mary to try to open a school for African-American children.

_____ **4.** Mary's sweet potato pies were the best ever made.

_____ **5.** Mary named the new school building Faith Hall.

Exploring Words

Write the correct word in each sentence.

attend	graduated	faith	depart	educate

1. To teach is to _____.

2. To go a school is to _____ it.

3. To leave is to _____.

4. Someone who has finished school has _____.

5. To believe that good things are possible is to have _____.

© Steck-Vaughn Company

Answer Key Nonfiction Grade 4

Assessments
P. 7
1. c
2. c
3. a
4. b
5. c
P. 8
Answers will vary.
P. 9
A. 4, 5, 1, 3, 2, 6
B. 1. opinion
2. fact
3. fact
4. opinion
P. 10
A. Answers may vary.
Examples:
1. she did not realize how serious the storm was.
2. icy snow drove into his face.
3. the wind threw him in.
4. they were frozen.
B. 1. true
2. false
3. false
4. true
5. false
Pp. 12-13
Do You Remember?
1. F
2. T
3. F
4. T
5. F
Express Yourself
Answers will vary.
Exploring Words
1. coffins
2. prevented
3. disease
4. department
5. foundlings
6. foster
7. mothering
8. cuddled
Pp. 15-16
Do You Remember?
1. T
2. T
3. T
4. F
5. T
Express Yourself
Answers will vary.
Exploring Words
1. in addition
2. equipment
3. immediately
4. minor
5. eternal
6. depth
7. amazement
8. opinion
9. bathyscaph
10. searchlight
Pp. 18-19
Do You Remember?
1. T
2. F
3. F

4. T
5. T
Critical Thinking
Answers may vary.
Examples:
1. he did not have any antitoxin and he was afraid the disease would kill everyone in town.
2. it was the closest town that had antitoxin.
3. of the winds and cold.
4. pieces of ice were stuck in their feet.
Exploring Words
1. a
2. b
3. a
4. a
5. c
6. c
7. b
8. a
Pp. 21-22
Do You Remember?
1. T
2. F
3. T
4. F
5. T
Express Yourself
Answers will vary.
Exploring Words
Across:
4. powerful
7. currents
8. mist
9. bobbing
Down:
1. life preservers
2. cruise
3. struggling
5. death
6. sandbar
Pp. 24-25
Do You Remember?
1. a
2. b
3. a
4. b
5. c
Critical Thinking
1. O
2. F
3. O
4. O
5. F
Exploring Words
1. stale
2. miners
3. spirits
4. survivors
5. violently
6. calm
7. miracle
8. delay
Pp. 27-28
Express Yourself
Answers will vary.
Do You Remember?
1. c
2. b

3. b
4. a
Exploring Words
1. smashed
2. slumped
3. frostbite
4. throbbed
5. cramps
6. contact
Pp. 30-31
Do You Remember?
1. c
2. b
3. c
4. b
5. b
Express Yourself
Answers will vary.
Exploring Words
1. runway
2. jammed
3. plunged
4. stunned
5. horror
6. off-duty
7. injured
8. released
9. clerk
10. sensed
Pp. 33-34
Express Yourself
Answers will vary.
Do You Remember?
1. b
2. a
3. c
4. a
Exploring Words
1. b
2. c
3. c
4. b
5. b
6. c
Pp. 36-37
Critical Thinking
1 and 3
Do You Remember?
1. T
2. T
3. F
4. T
Exploring Words
Across:
2. vitamin C
7. passage
8. request
Down:
1. rare
3. criminals
4. Majesty
5. anchor
6. spice
Pp. 39-40
Do You Remember?
1. c
2. a
3. c
Critical Thinking
1. F
2. O

3. F
4. O
Exploring Words
1. self-powered
2. principles
3. gliders
4. curves
5. gently
6. span
7. propeller
Pp. 42-43
Do You Remember?
1. T
2. F
3. T
4. T
Express Yourself
Answers will vary.
Exploring Words
Across:
2. layer
5. exhausted
6. trudged
7. frostbite
8. igloo
9. underneath
Down:
1. position
3. Arctic
4. expedition
7. frigid
Pp. 45-46
Critical Thinking
4, 5, 2, 3, 1
Do You Remember?
1. c
2. c
3. a
4. a
Exploring Words
1. official
2. tides
3. battered
4. currents
5. swollen
6. energy
Pp. 48-49
Express Yourself
Answers will vary.
Do You Remember?
1. F
2. F
3. T
4. F
5. T
Exploring Words
1. c
2. b
3. b
4. c
5. a
6. a
Pp. 51-52
Do You Remember?
1. F
2. T
3. T
4. T
5. T

Answer Key Nonfiction Grade 4 (p. 2)

Critical Thinking
1. O
2. F
3. F
4. O
5. F
Exploring Words
1. reporter
2. editor
3. boasted
4. imaginary
5. seasick
6. overboard
7. informed
8. failure
Pp. 54-55
Critical Thinking
2, 5, 1, 4, 3
Do You Remember?
1. c
2. b
3. a
4. c
Exploring Words
1. chorus
2. film
3. familiar
4. presently
5. personality
6. resist
Pp. 57-58
Do You Remember?
1. b
2. c
3. b
4. a
5. b
Express Yourself
Answers will vary.
Exploring Words
1. research
2. fakes
3. abominable
4. filmed
5. mysterious
6. reared
7. gorilla
8. scrambled
9. claim
10. described
Pp. 60-61
Do You Remember?
1. c
2. c
3. b
4. c
Critical Thinking
2 and 3
Exploring Words
1. monster
2. murky
3. hump
4. existed
5. imagination
6. sonar
7. fantastic
Pp. 63-64
Critical Thinking
2

Do You Remember?
1. a
2. b
3. a
4. c
Exploring Words
1. urge
2. haunted
3. lurking
4. solid
5. evil
6. presence
7. murder
8. inflict
Pp. 66-67
Express Yourself
Answers will vary.
Do You Remember?
1. a
2. b
3. a
4. c
Exploring Words
1. a
2. c
3. a
4. c
5. b
6. b
Pp. 69-70
Do You Remember?
1. b
2. b
3. a
4. b
5. c
Critical Thinking
4, 3, 2, 1
Exploring Words
1. submarine
2. survive
3. Barnacles
4. torpedo
5. attract
6. shark
Pp. 72-73
Express Yourself
Answers will vary.
Do You Remember?
1. T
2. T
3. F
4. T
5. F
Exploring Words
1. slumped
2. microphone
3. runway
4. controls
5. gear
Pp. 75-76
Do You Remember?
1. b
2. a
3. b
4. a
5. a
Critical Thinking
Answers may vary.

Examples:
1. he wanted to warn them about the fire.
2. a lookout thought the fire was in a different place.
3. they were trying to get away from the fire.
Exploring Words
1. fiercely
2. lantern
3. fled
4. embers
5. shingles
6. acres
Pp. 78-79
Do You Remember?
1. T
2. F
3. T
4. F
5. T
Express Yourself
Answers will vary.
Exploring Words
1. a
2. a
3. b
4. a
5. a
6. c
7. a
8. b
Pp. 81-82
Do You Remember?
1. F
2. T
3. T
4. F
5. T
Express Yourself
Answers will vary.
Exploring Words
Across:
2. photographer
6. binoculars
7. volcano
9. mask
10. logger
Down:
1. erupt
3. helicopter
4. powerful
5. wasteland
8. average
Pp. 84-85
Critical Thinking
3, 1, 4, 2
Do You Remember?
1. T
2. F
3. T
4. T
5. T
Exploring Words
1. Events
2. officials
3. threatened
4. weapon
5. naturally

Pp. 87-88
Critical Thinking
2, 4, 1, 3
Do You Remember?
1. a
2. c
3. b
4. b
5. c
Exploring Words
1. pirate
2. spared
3. rejoiced
4. terrified
5. governor
6. demanded
Pp. 90-91
Critical Thinking
Answers may vary.
Examples:
1. many factory owners kept their doors locked and the workers could not escape.
2. she ordered them to stop using child workers.
Do You Remember?
1. c
2. b
3. a
4. b
5. c
Exploring Words
1. a
2. b
3. a
4. c
5. c
Pp. 93-94
Do You Remember?
1. b
2. a
3. b
4. a
Critical Thinking
1. F
2. F
3. O
4. O
5. F
Exploring Words
1. educate
2. attend
3. depart
4. graduated
5. faith

© Steck-Vaughn Company